SOLVING THE WEALTH PUZZLE

THE RICH DIDN'T GET WEALTHY IN THE STOCK MARKET—YOU WON'T EITHER!

DEBUNKING THE MYTHS, LIES, AND HALF-TRUTHS OF CREATING WEALTH IN AMERICA

ANTHONY DEEMER

IUNIVERSE, INC.
NEW YORK   BLOOMINGTON

Solving the Wealth Puzzle
The Rich Didn't Get Wealthy in the Stock
Market— You Won't Either!

iUniverse books may be ordered through booksellers or by contacting:

iUniverse
1663 Liberty Drive
Bloomington, IN 47403
www.iuniverse.com
1-800-Authors (1-800-288-4677)

Because of the dynamic nature of the Internet, any Web addresses or links contained in this book may have changed since publication and may no longer be valid. The views expressed in this work are solely those of the author and do not necessarily reflect the views of the publisher, and the publisher hereby disclaims any responsibility for them.

ISBN: 978-0-595-44444-1 (sc)
ISBN: 978-0-595-88770-5 (ebk)

Printed in the United States of America

iUniverse rev. date: 10/19/2009

This book is dedicated to my family. Without the love and support they have given me, it could not have been written.

CONTENTS

ACKNOWLEDGMENTS

I owe a special thanks to my longtime friend and business partner Gray Hudson for lending me his invaluable twenty-five years of experience in the investment industry and his assistance in the research for this book.

Thanks also to Anne Wayman for guiding this manuscript with her professional editing and the facilitating of all the publishing arrangements.

I would also like to thank Christopher Rizzo for his technical support and marketing designs.

FOREWORD

By Gray Hudson

Wake up, America! Now!

Sometime during the summer of 2006, the population of the United States of America reached the milestone of three hundred million people. As I reflected on that noteworthy achievement I wondered about the future of our society. Are we better off today than our parents or grandparents? What will the future hold for our children and the generations to come?

Today, Americans have more material goods than their forefathers did, but we seem to enjoy them less and less. Most of us spend our waking hours working to get ahead in hopes of creating sufficient wealth to buy time for ourselves at retirement, but live in fear, and rightly so, that whatever we earn won't be enough. More and more we complain about how fast time is passing and how little time we have.

We are born into this world, go to school, graduate, find a job, work toward retirement, and then we die. Our tombstone might read, "He was born, he lived, and he died."

We don't understand the mess we're in, so we look for someone to blame. We blame our parents, grandparents, the schools and teachers, the church, the government, radio, TV, newspapers, magazines, books, and movies for all our problems. As a result of all that blaming, it rarely occurs to us to take real responsibility for our own lives.

It wasn't like this a generation or two ago—in the past; people stood up on their own two feet and persevered, no excuses. People were tough back then because there were not any options. They either figured out a way to get it done or they died.

The changes in attitude probably began as the country moved into the industrial revolution in the early 1900s. It was then that some companies found it helpful to offer some workers deferred compensation in the form of pensions—money paid to the worker upon their retirement.

In 1935, what we refer to today as Social Security was implemented as one response to the depression. Social Security was designed to help fund the gap between the times a person's work life ended and their death.[1]

When we look at our fairly recent history, we discover that major pushes for pensions and other benefits, like employer-paid health insurance, were designed to help companies find employees when wages were frozen during World War II.[2]

In the last decade or so, benefits enlarged to include products like 401(k)s, where employers matched all or some of the employee's contributions to a retirement fund.

All of this has led people to believe a lie that says, "You are not responsible for funding your own retirement."

The last few generations have grown up believing that all you need to do is get a good job with benefits, because sticking with the job means not having to plan and save for retirement, as it would be taken care of by the company and the government.

Admittedly, encouraging people not to save for their own retirement freed up spending as people purchased additional goods and services with the money they might have, under other circumstances, saved. For a long while this drove the economy, creating jobs and general prosperity.

The only problem with this is that while it worked for a few decades, times are changing. Baby Boomers began to turn sixty in 2006, and as this large segment of the population moves into retirement and old age, they will place an added strain on programs and services. Spiraling healthcare costs and other economic issues are forcing more and more companies to drop pension plans in order to compete.

Social Security, the "Third Rail" in politics, is coming under pressure to meet obligations it was never designed to face. When most pensions and Social Security were created, the average life expectancy was sixty-six years of age. Today, the fastest growing segment of the population is over the age of ninety-five. Social Security and pension plans were designed for a shorter life span—the funding for the extended life expectancy simply is not there.

To make matters worse, the generations that follow the Baby Boomers, the Gen-Xs and Gen-Ys, are smaller in size and sadly underemployed. Yet they too have been brought up with the myth that they don't need to save for retirement because the government and their employers will do their saving for them.

According to government estimates, Medicare will be out of money by 2018 and by 2040 Social Security will only be able to pay 74 percent of the scheduled annual benefits.[3]

Have you checked to see what your Social Security benefits will actually amount to? You should. You can ask the Social Security Administration to give you an estimate by calling your local office. You can also get the information from their Web site: http://www.ssa.gov/.

Once you get your estimate, ask yourself, "Can I live on 74 percent of that?" My guess is it won't even come close to covering you in retirement.

This means your kids and your grandkids are going to be SOL.

It gets worse. Corporate America is racing to get out from under their future pension obligations. The government's Pension Guarantee Corporation is getting bled dry by under funded pensions and gross mismanagement.

Friends, I am not running around pulling this fire alarm for shits and grins—this is serious. What do you think is going to happen when everyone shows up at retirement with their hands out and a sad story about why they didn't save any money?

If you think that people only spend a few years in retirement, guess again. According to life insurance mortality tables, a male who reaches age sixty-five has a fifty-fifty chance of living to age eighty-five. If you are a woman, the odds are even better.[4] But Americans, not surprisingly, are notoriously poor savers and save less than people of any other developed country.

If pensions no longer exist, Social Security runs out of money, and Medicare goes broke, what will happen to you? It depends on what you do now.

The first question you want to ask yourself is, "How much money I will need in retirement to be comfortable?"

That's easy to answer. Just take your current monthly income (say five thousand dollars) and multiply it by 80 percent (hope the kids are out of the house and you have paid down your mortgage). Next, figure out how inflation will affect that total. Just to be on the safe side, use 4 percent per year for inflation. That means in order to get the four-thousand-dollars-a-month buying power you have today, you will need eight thousand dollars a month in about eighteen years.

Given the increasing life expectancy, you need to plan on being retired for as many years as you were working, especially if you are married. You will want to protect your retirement money by withdrawing only about 4 percent of your account balance each year, which allows your money to replenish itself. So if you need eight thousand dollars by the time you retire in eighteen years, you will need to have saved two million dollars for retirement. Yes, that's two million dollars. It's just that simple.

So where are you going to get two million dollars in the next eighteen years or so? That's the whole point of this book.

There will soon be two types of people in America—the haves and the have-nots. Middle-income America is vanishing. What does that mean for the future of our society? You will fall into one of two categories … either rich or poor.

Now that I have your attention, I'll bet you are thinking about your own personal situation and where you stand. In your own defense you are probably saying something like, "Yes, but you don't know my world and the problems I face. I do a good job with what I make, but it's just not enough."

Listen up. The sooner you address this issue the better. Savings in America today are at a *negative* 1 percent.[5] Most Americans are up to their eyeballs in debt and are still reaching for that next credit card application that came in the mail.

You have two choices:

- Cut back on your spending.
- Increase your income.

While it is certainly possible for most people to save some money, (a quick internet search will give you all sorts of ideas), saving two million dollars over the next eighteen or twenty years is impossible. Why? Because it would take you twenty years with an average rate of return of 8 percent per year and a investment of fifty thousand dollars each year to reach the goal of 2.1 million dollars in savings.

If saving money out of your current income won't work, the other option is to increase your income. What would happen if you go to work tomorrow and ask for a raise? Even if you are given one, how much will it be? If you saved every single nickel of that raise, would it add up to the two million dollars you need? Highly unlikely.

What about the equity in your house, if you own a home? It will help, but get real here too. Even if you manage to retire when the real estate market is good, how much can you actually expect if you sell? Probably nothing close to two million dollars and you will still need a place to live.

What are your real options? The stock market? Read on and you will find out why that won't work. In fact, there is only one solution that offers you the biggest and most realistic chance of creating the two million dollars you will need, and even more.

Read on!

Gray Hudson

INTRODUCTION

Have you ever been in a position where you had to make a decision to do the right thing even though it might cost you? You know what I mean—where doing the right thing might cost you your job or a friendship. I have been in this position more than once in my life. Being in this uncomfortable position will make you check your principles and look at who you really are.

I have spent the last ten years in the investment industry as an investment advisor, and I find myself back in that position of doing the right thing. In this book my goal is to share with you how stockbrokers and investment companies actually view you as a client. I want you to know about the hidden agendas most investment advisors have when they pitch you on a stock. It's not pretty.

You see, if an advisor is not careful, the investment industry will seduce him or her with the lure of seven figure incomes, expensive cars, and Rolex watches.

Wall Street is a greed-driven machine, and it doesn't matter what company your advisor works for, because sooner or later he or she will be asked to compromise his or her principles.

I have watched new college graduates try to deal with this dilemma in their first three weeks of training. Because the industry is driven by commission payouts, sales quotas, and company bottom lines, the new advisor is told to sell one particular product over another to a client, and the majority of the time it is because product A pays a higher commission than product B. In other words, advisors are not born to do the wrong thing for their client. The industry's big-name companies actually teach advisors to favor fees and commissions over the benefit of the client.

I have attended conferences with over one thousand advisors in attendance and have overheard conversations like, "I love this business because I make money when my clients make money, and I make money when my clients lose money."

I want you to understand that what you are being told by the big-name investment companies, the financial news media, and most trained advisors is an absolute lie. The idea that you are going to get rich by investing in the stock market is the biggest lie being told today in America.

Based on my experience as an advisor and years of researching for this book, I can tell you that the rich have not built, and nor are they building, their wealth by investing in the stock market. The truth is the rich do not like the stock market for one big reason: they have no control. The wealthy understand that as consumers we have no control over what the market will do. The rich understand investing in the stock market is really gambling and are not comfortable with someone else gambling with their money. So they would rather invest their money elsewhere.

In this book I share with you how the rich in this country built their wealth and how they continue to do so.

This book was not written with the intention to sell a get-rich-quick system. I think we have enough of these types of products in the market now. No, the intention of this book is to share with you the truth behind how the rich in this country are building their wealth and to let you know what Wall Street is not telling you.

I want to help change the way we think in this country. I want people to realize that what we have been told for the past twenty to thirty years about how to build financial security will no longer work.

In the past we have been told that if we finish high school, go to college, get a degree, and get a job we will be secure.

Now let's look at that formula for a moment and consider how many news stories tell us about companies like Ford, which according to USA Today decided to cut twenty-five thousand to thirty thousand jobs and close fourteen plants in 2006,[6] or tell us how many jobs are being outsourced overseas.

You have to realize that there is no such thing as job security anymore, and following the formula mentioned above will take you down the path of financial failure.

As a nation we have to wake up, stop sticking our heads in the sand, and stop thinking that things are going to get better or change. The truth is that we are living in a different time than our parents or grandparents' did, and the sooner you realize that the better off you and your family will be.

When I first began writing this book, I had no idea of how it would change my life. Once I started my research I was in absolute amazement and asked myself why I hadn't seen this before now—it had been right in front of my eyes all along.

The secret to building wealth is no secret—it is in front us everyday, and in this book you will learn that secret.

The problem is that we have been brainwashed into thinking in a different way, into believing in the old formula of:

Good Job = Security

Because of this we are blind to the other investment options available for building wealth.

I wrote this book with the intention that, by the time you finish it, there will be no question in your mind about how to build wealth for yourself. If, after reading this book you decide that becoming rich isn't for you, that's okay, but you will not be able say you don't know how.

Anthony Deemer

CHAPTER 1

THE STOCK MARKET WILL NOT MAKE YOU RICH

When money speaks, the truth keeps silent.
Russian Proverb

Have you ever wondered how the millionaires in this country made their money? Contrary to popular belief, *the richest people in America* did not *accumulate their wealth by investing in the stock market.*

Considering the amount of media coverage that the stock market gets on a daily basis and the billions spent on advertising by Wall Street firms, it is not at all surprising if you have come away with the impression that you can start out with very little money and strike it rich by investing it in the market. Unfortunately, this is largely a fabrication.

There are three reasons why it is almost impossible to consistently make money in the stock market:

1. **Investors are driven by their emotions.** For the most part, investors decide to buy or sell based on two emotions: fear and greed. You have only to look at the Enron and WorldCom fiascos to see that this is true. Or, you can follow any stock market report over a period of weeks or months

1

and verify for yourself that stock prices rise and fall based on rumors and guesstimates rather than real facts and clear thinking.

While it is true that investors who follow the old sayings below increase the odds in their favor, it doesn't really matter because the market rises and falls in totally unpredictable ways.

- Buy low, sell high
- Recognize that stocks are a long-term investment
- Make sure to diversify their portfolios

Imagine what happens if the stock market is on a slide when you need to sell.

2. **To win big in the stock market you have to start with a lot of money.** Another way to say this is, "It's easy to become a millionaire in the stock market—just start with a million dollars."

   The truth is it takes an initial investment of at least one hundred thousand dollars to win big in the market, and even then there are no guarantees. There are no guarantees because even with a sizeable investment you have no control over what the companies you invest in actually do. For example, how many investors in the Big Three auto companies do you suppose would have advised them to get into fuel-efficient vehicles years ago? Yet until very recently these companies have ignored the issue and are in serious trouble as a result.

The stock market industry talks a lot about how a small investor can get rich by investing just fifty dollars a month. But the truth is you would have to invest fifty dollars a month at a rate of return of ten percent per year for a full fifty-two years to make your first million. That means if you started at age thirty-five, you would be eighty-seven by the time you became a millionaire—and that does not include the taxes you will owe on the profits. Are you willing to wait fifty-seven years? I don't think so.

3. **The stock market is designed to benefit the rich and the brokerage firms that sell investments, not the small investor.** Stockbrokers and brokerage houses make their money on the commissions and fees they charge each time they sell or buy investments for their clients. The larger the transaction, the bigger their commissions and fees, which is why so many are now limiting their client base to those who have one hundred thousand dollars or even more to invest.

In fact, the people who are already rich have access to alternative and more lucrative investment products that the average Jane and Joe will never see, like Private REITs, Hedge Funds, and Private Equity.

In other words, in spite of the fancy ads, glossy PR, and the attempt to generate excitement or gloom during stock market reports, the odds are stacked against the small investor. The advertising tries to control what you think, how you feel, and your attitudes and perceptions about the stock market. Ads are designed to get you to create buy-and-sell orders, which generate transaction fees and profits for the brokerage firms.

Market insiders know that they are selling legalized gambling. They understand that the biggest casino in the world is not in Las Vegas or Atlantic City—it is Wall Street. At least when you go to Las Vegas, Atlantic City, or any casino or even buy a lottery ticket, you know that the odds are in favor of the house. They couldn't be in business if this were not true. When you gamble you know what you are getting into.

Although few realize it, the same thing is true of the stock market—the odds are in favor of the house, which is Wall Street, not you.

> *The long view shows why diversification is overrated …*
>
> —Roger Lowenstein, *Smart Money,* February 2007

Marketing the Market

But Wall Street does not emphasize the gambling nature of the stock market—far from it. Instead they use a façade of legitimacy. Everything you read, see, and hear about the stock market is designed to present it as an opportunity rather than gambling. It is done simply by making the newspaper columnists, article writers, talk show hosts, ex-stock jockeys, bloggers, and others seem like experts.

What they never tell you is that their "experts" are gambling with your money—they are betting that stocks will go up or down—and for the brokers and dealers, it is a sure bet because they have it both ways. What is rarely spelled out clearly is that no matter which way the market goes, they win because they make money every time someone buys or sells, regardless of the losses or gains of the buyers and sellers.

Wall Street is just like any other industry. Millions are spent on psychologists, focus groups, and behavioral specialists in order to discover how they can sell their products and services. The big difference is in what they are selling. It's not like they are trying to sell

> In 2006, stockholders sued some 120 companies for one form or another of fraud involving stock, according to a report in *The Sun Sentinel*

you the latest bottled water, a new car, or a teeth whitener. Instead, they are selling a fantasy disguised as an investment in corporate America.

The way Wall Street creates an aura of respectability is through their so-called experts—fund analysts, stockbrokers, financial advisors, and others—who then try to make people think they know what they're talking about. These experts are positioned to make people think that they can outsmart the market.

One of the most obvious and effective approaches is for the experts to pitch *the next big thing* before anyone else knows about it. The experts may actually believe what they are saying because their brokers and the companies they work for get them to buy into this line of thinking.

But it is common knowledge in the industry that *no one can predict what the market will do next.*

MAKING A MARKET

Brokerage firms often create or make a market. It works like this:

1. A brokerage firm buys a large block of stock in a certain company they think has growth potential.
2. To make a profit, the firm has to sell this stock for more than they bought it.
3. The word goes out to all the firm's stockbrokers to push the stock on to their clients, which creates increased buying activity.
4. The increased buying activity causes a higher demand in that stock and the stock price rises.
5. Competing brokerage firms see that something is happening and play "follow the herd" with more buy orders which cause the share price to go even higher.

6. Once the original brokerage firm has sold all of its holdings at a nice profit, the push stops and the inflated share price falls.
7. Falling share prices trigger a sell-off and the brokerage firm wins again by receiving transaction fees on the sell orders.

In other words, the brokerage firm created the buzz that allowed them to collect commissions both as their clients bought on the original push and again when the selling began.

It is almost impossible for an individual investor to recognize when such a scheme is in operation. Consumers have been taught to rely on the advice of their brokers and are often the worse off because of it.

IT AIN'T PREDICTABLE

Simply put, it is not possible to predict the stock market. *You* cannot predict the market. *I* cannot predict it. *No one* can, not even the experts. Anyone who tells you otherwise is a liar! There are so many factors involved that forecasting what the stock market will do is impossible.

Here are just six of the factors that influence the market:

1. The market is made up of companies that are run by CEOs whose decisions and actions affect the profitability or lack thereof of their companies. Remember Enron, WorldCom, and now Hewlett Packard? In each case, the CEO made decisions that resulted in disaster—those decisions were not predictable.
2. It is an unpredictable world, and world events have a huge influence on the market—if you have any doubts, consider what happened to the market following September 11, 2001. The stock

market never opened on 9/11 and remained closed for the next four trading sessions. When the market opened again on 9/17, the Dow fell 684.71 points.

3. The unforeseeable rise in price of a needed product affects the market. Remember what happened to oil prices following Hurricane Katrina.

4. Hurricanes are not the only weather events that have largely unpredictable but significant influences on the market. A drought, a flood, or unexpected cold or heat often creates havoc in stock prices.

5. Negative media coverage about a company's products or key officers often affects the market. So do rumors on the Internet.

6. Government policies and politics often have unpredictable consequences on the price of shares.

Each of the above market influences, and there are many more, are instances where fear and greed kick in and cause people to buy and/or sell. Exactly how people will react to any given situation is unpredictable, and hence the market is unpredictable by any measure.

Yet the people who call themselves "market experts" continue to give all sorts of advice, presenting the impression that somehow they can foresee the future and forecast what the market will do.

NOTICE THE DISCLAIMERS!

Of course, all this advice is coached with caution that shows up in the form of disclaimers. Taking into account all the disclaimers about the risk of investing plastered on everything investors are asked to read and sign, it is a wonder anyone invests in the stock market. Yet over and over again people decide one stockbroker, some fund manager, or other expert has some special insight about what the market will do next. The result for the individual is often major losses—losses you do not hear about because they are not considered newsworthy.

AN EXPERIMENT

Richard Wiseman of the University of Hertfordshire in England did an experiment in which three imaginary portfolios were set up with an initial stake of five thousand dollars.

1. In one portfolio he had a professional stock analyst pick the stocks.
2. In another, an astrologer made the choice based on the movement of the stars and planets.
3. A five-year-old girl picked the stocks for the third portfolio.

Then he waited for a year. At the end of that year the results showed that the professional stock analyst's picks went down 46.2 percent, the astrologer's portfolio went down 6.2 percent, and the five-year-old girl came out ahead of everyone, with a growth rate of 5.8 percent. That's right—a five-year-old girl actually picked winning stocks, although a 5.8 percent growth rate isn't all that high.[7] So much for the experts' ability to predict the market.

PICKING STOCKS IS NOT THEIR JOB

The so-called experts are not good at picking stocks. In fact, picking stocks is not even their job. They are really salespeople trained in the art of pushing stock products for a commission.

If you think that you are making a smart decision by choosing an advisor or broker based on the number of years they have been in the business, think again. It doesn't matter if the advisor has twenty years or five minutes of experience, they always have their own agenda, which, is to get you to buy and sell one way or another so they can make a commission.

A broker once said that, "I love the investment industry because I don't care if my clients made money or lost it—I made money either way."

Could this be your stockbroker?

How Wall Street Really Works

Wall Street is geared toward the institutional money manager pensions and the mutual fund industry. Why? Because that is where the bulk of the money is.

Consider this: Wall Street controls over eight trillion dollars of retirement money through the mutual fund industry.[8] And for every one percent the money manager's charge, they are able to stick another eight billion dollars in their pockets—the eight billion is what the one-percent fee adds up to.

Mutual fund companies spend a lot of time courting broker-dealers through fancy dinners and golf outings with the intention of getting rich off of their controlled sales force—the stockbrokers, fund advisors, financial planners, etc. Everyone charges their customers fees, and the broker-dealers also keep a part of each commission charged to the customer. They know that the way to make more money for them is to make more trades in their clients' accounts.

Every time a trade is made, the broker-dealer and the stockbroker make money from the trading fees charged and the commissions paid. Both figures are based on a percentage of the amount traded. The larger the trade, the higher the profit.

Broker-dealers are constantly pushing their stockbrokers and other representatives to present new investment products and stocks to their clients to maximize the amount of transactions executed.

When I first started out in the financial planning industry, this business of commissions and fees based on the size of a transaction was always troubling for my family and me. I was never comfortable selling products to clients knowing it was not in their best interest. As an investment advisor with a big financial company, whose name I won't mention but who was part of the credit card company industry, I was always asked to sell their mutual funds to my clients even though the funds had a horrible track record on their returns. The company simply didn't care about results—they were only interested in my recommendation to my clients that they buy the company's mutual funds.[9]

In the past I have seen advisors push one product over another because it paid a higher commission or because pressure from upper management was so great that they went ahead and sold the product out of fear of loosing their job.

Obviously, brokers and dealers want to keep as much money in the market as possible. If instead that money went into savings or real estate, the brokers would not profit from it over and over again as they do now when moving clients from one stock to another. They currently do their research not on what the various companies are actually doing but on what product will appeal to the public. What is hot, sexy, and exciting at the moment is what sells, and there are huge profits to be made by peddling the next fad to investors.

> *The tech industry has been turned on its head ... as scores of companies have come under fire for engaging in the illegal practice of stock options "backdating."* EDN. com January 2007.

Remember how tech stocks were pushed in the 1990s? The public was just catching on to the Internet and the World Wide Web. Venture capitalists were funding start-ups regardless of their business model. Many of these start-ups went public even when no one, including the founders, had any idea of how the company would make money.

As soon as a new company went public, investors were urged to buy their stock. Then investors were urged to buy another new stock, often selling the original high-tech stocks in the process. This happened over and over and over again.

A whole new stock index for tech stocks was designed (NASDAQ) and promoted. Pension plans and mutual funds joined the speculation and the race was on. It was during this period that day trading became popular.

Suddenly, the dotcom boom went bust. Millions of people lost significant amounts of money and many found themselves broke. But not the brokerage houses. The brokerage houses made money as people bought into the dotcom boom, and they made more money as people and institutions bailed out and tried to minimize their losses.

In the trade, it is called "feeding the monster," and the market truly is a monster. When an investment firm is designing a product or compiling a list of stocks to sell, you can be certain the firm will choose those that will make them the most money.

IF THEY ARE SO GOOD ...

If you have a stockbroker or other financial expert who recommends stocks, or if you 'have ever talked with one, ask yourself this: if that stockbroker really had a way to make all that money quickly and easily, don't you think they would have already made it and would now be sitting on some beach somewhere watching the sun go down? I know I would, and I suspect you would too.

If they really had the hot hand in the market, why are they still working for someone else? If they are as good as they say, why aren't they rich and retired? If their system actually worked, don't you think people would be beating a path to their door? Why are you still seeing their ads running on TV and in the newspaper?

The next time a stockbroker tells you they have a winning or hot stock, ask them how many shares they are buying. Do not be surprised at the answer ... none. That is, if you get an answer at all. Generally, brokers do not buy many of the stocks they recommend, which tells you something about how the market really works.

Why Wall Street Won't Work for You

What is it that Wall Street is not telling us? What is the *inside secret* they do not want you to know? What is the *truth* behind all the advertising you see every day? Here it is—a list of the reasons why the stock market won't work for you:

1. **You have no control.** The market goes up and down whether you are holding, buying, selling, or diversifying.
2. **You don't have enough information.** The key to buying and selling stocks is timely and complete information from a number of related sources. Making timely decisions requires complete information and daily attention, and even then nothing is certain.
3. **You do not have enough start-up capital.** You cannot invest successfully if you have no money, only a small amount, or by putting a few dollars away over time. It takes money to make money.
4. **You are all alone.** Unless you hire a broker or pay for a "Personal Stock Guide Service," you are making all the decisions by yourself. Are you qualified to do that? The answer is obvious.
5. **You have a job.** Stock picking is not a part-time job—it is not even a nine-to-five job. Things happen all the time that affect the value of your stocks. While you are sleeping, other stock markets around the world are opening up and getting started for the day. It is truly a global industry. It is too easy to find out the next morning that

what London did last night meant you should have sold before dawn.

6. **Your brokerage has no loyalty to you.** A what-have-you-done-for-me-lately attitude is pervasive throughout the brokerage community. (And "lately" actually means in the last hour or so.) This leads to insecurity and instability in the ranks of the salespeople. Pressure from the top causes actions that are made for the firm's bottom line and not for yours. Brokers are being squeezed from both competition and the upper management, which means something has to give, and usually the thing that gives is respect for the customer.

7. **The market will do what the market will do.** Putting all your money in the stock market is a recipe for failure. No one can predict what it will do next, and as the fine print on *all* investment literature says: *past performance is not a guarantee of future results.*

   Whatever your stockbroker may have told you, the fine-print disclaimer says it all. Just because stocks went up most of the time in the past century does not mean they will not go down most of the time in this one. If you think you can invest in the market and do nothing else, you are wrong.

8. **You do not have the access.** You do not have the access or the money to get into the really good investments that the ultra-rich are privy to. The lower you are on the totem pole the worse off you are in terms of access. As a result, you are left with the crumbs.

9. **You are being lied to.** The investment returns that the industry claims are untruths and even

outright lies. When you calculate inflation and fees and subtract these from the returns, your profits dwindle to nothing.

According to a February 2006 article in the Wall Street Journal, a study done by Thornburg Investment Management found that Wall Street gives the public inflated numbers to make their returns look better. The mutual fund companies tell the public that if they had invested one dollar in the S&P 500 at the start of 1926 that they would have had $2,655.73 at the end of December 2005. In fact, if you calculate the *real* return (adjusting for the effects of inflation, taxes, and trading expenses), that original dollar would only be worth $46.59! That's a *big* difference![10]

For years, Wall Street and the media have spouted that fortunes can be made by investing in the market. People buy tons of books, attend countless costly meeting and seminars, and spend thousands of hours researching online, all in the pursuit of trying to get rich through investing in the stock market. And still with all that, you would be hard pressed to find someone—if anyone—who made themselves rich by investing only in stocks and bonds.

Why is that? The answer can be stated in one word: *control.* You cannot control the market. It is out of your hands.

Experts like to say, "If you own a stock, then you are an owner of the company." But that is not true. Even as a stockholder you do not have a say in the day-to-day operations, you cannot fire an employee for showing up late, and you cannot force a change in management. Sure, you do get to vote on certain company issues, but those votes do not have much, if any, influence on the way a company behaves. You do not have any say on how much should be spent on marketing or even how much is spent on coffee in the break room.

Plus, if the company goes out of business, as a stockholder you are last on the list to get any money back. In fact, you are likely to get nothing at all. Just look at the investors who had their money invested with companies like Enron, WorldCom, Kmart, Pan American, and Eastern airlines. Thousands of individual investors and almost as many employees who had invested their 401(k)s in company stocks were wiped out. None of these stockholders had even a tiny bit of control—and you don't either.

WHAT IS REALLY TRUE

The average American today, according to Laura Bruce at Bankrate.com, saves less than they did twenty years ago. Laura Bruce stated that in May of 1985 Americans saved 11.1 percent of their disposable income, and in 2005 Americans spent more than they earned, creating a negative savings rate of 0.5 percent.[11] The National Sleep Foundation conducted their "Sleep in America" poll for 2005, and respondents said they worked an average of forty-seven hours per week. It is no wonder people are looking for a way to get more, go faster, keep pace, and stay ahead of the game.

To get rich you need to be in control, and you need to be able to make the decisions that will lead you to financial success. As we have shown in this chapter, you have no control in the stock market.

So you may be asking yourself, how did wealthy people in America become rich? This book will show you the true path to riches.

CHAPTER 2

THE TRUE PATH TO WEALTH

Do not go where the path may lead, go instead where there is no path and leave a trail.
Ralph Waldo Emerson

If the stock market is not the path to wealth, what is? The answer may surprise you. Simply put, the most reliable path to getting rich is … starting and owning your own business.

Yes, entrepreneurship is the real key to becoming rich. The statistics prove this to be true:

- According to CNNMoney.com's Jeanne Sahadi, research compiled by the Spectrem Group found that the number of U.S. households with a net worth of at least one million dollars, excluding primary homes, grew to nine million.[12]
- According to an article in the *New York Times*, two thirds of millionaires in the United States are self-employed.
- According to economist Edward Wolff of New York University, the lion's share of our country's wealth has gone to the top one percent of the population—people worth three million dollars

or more. The biggest part of their income comes from businesses they own.[13]

- The Small Business Administration says entrepreneurial businesses account for 99.7 percent of our nation's employers, 54 percent of its employees, and 52 percent of sales. [14]
- The Federal Reserve Board found that between 1992 and 2001, the average net worth of households headed by self-employed people rose from $714,500 to 1.2 million dollars, a level five times greater than "the average working household.[15]

If you want to become a millionaire or better, you have to stop working for someone else and start working for yourself. That means becoming an entrepreneur and having your own business.

WHY WORKING FOR OTHERS DOES NOT WORK

Most of us have been brought up with the idea that we will work for other people. In most cases, that is the model our parents set, even if they were not happy in their job and even if their employment meant there was not much money in the family.

I can still hear my parents saying, "Study hard and get good grades so you can get into college. You can't get a good job without a college degree." The goal was the job and only the job.

Schools, including high schools, trade schools, and colleges, reinforce the idea that when we graduate we will get a job working for a company or working for someone other than ourselves. In fact, many schools also teach job-hunting skills, showing students how to prepare resumes, write cover letters, and search the internet for jobs. Effort is always aimed at helping students get jobs

It used to be that if you worked hard and played by the rules, you'd be okay. But that's no longer true. For many people, the American dream is eroding ...
—William D. Novelli, CEO AARP

with some company or another—always setting them up to work for someone else.

The possibilities and opportunities of self-employment are almost never mentioned, let alone discussed. Instead it is simply assumed that the way to go is to get a job.

Our education system, the media, and our society in general have programmed us to think that the path to prosperity is paved with a college degree and a corporate job. But this model is obsolete. What they are really preparing you for is failure and a life of poverty.

It is rather strange, because if you study the history of our country you will find that since its founding, building wealth has almost always been achieved through entrepreneurship. Consider these three founders:

> 1. Ben Franklin is a prime example. With his printing press and scientific experiments, he offers an excellent model of self-employment.
> 2. George Washington learned surveying by apprenticing to a surveyor and then quickly struck out on his own.
> 3. Thomas Jefferson also became a surveyor. In addition, he ran his own plantation and studied and then practiced law, opening up what today we would consider his own law office.

Back then, people saw a need and then started a business to fill that need. It was not until the early nineteenth century, when the industrial revolution was well established in this country, that people began to think working for someone else was a good idea.

The truth is, working for yourself is just as good an idea today as it was so long ago. In fact, it may be a better idea today. Because of today's uncertainty in the job market, entrepreneurship allows you to take control of your future.

Of course, as the statistics show, many people are self-employed or become what we call "Wealth Rebels." We will tell you more about becoming a Wealth Rebel as we go along.

TODAY'S JOB MARKET

If the statistics on how people get wealthy do not convince you to start your own business, today's job market should. The days of working for the same company for thirty years and retiring with a pension and a gold watch are long gone. In fact, someone just starting out today in the job market can expect to change jobs at least 9.6 times by the time they are thirty-six.[16]

Companies that have problems making a profit, for whatever the reason, try to improve their bottom line with layoffs. Wall Street often rewards companies making layoffs with higher stock prices. Obviously, neither the companies nor Wall Street are concerned about the laid-off employees. Small wonder the increasing layoff rate is downright frightening.

In September 2006, Intel announced it anticipated at least 10,500 layoffs by mid-2007. Ford Motor Company announced layoffs of 25,000 - 30,000 in January of 2006.

If you have not been laid off yourself, you probably know at least one person who has lost a job through downsizing, outsourcing, or just plain poor company management. You may know people who have lost more than one job that way.

For most, it is not a matter of if, but when they will be laid off. Why wait until you lose your job? Why not start your own business and quit on your own terms?

Even those who get to keep their jobs are finding their wages are not keeping up with inflation, their health insurance costs are skyrocketing, and the chances of receiving a pension are almost nonexistent. Companies are cutting back on benefits to help keep a lid on costs and to improve their bottom line. Fewer companies are offering pension plans, while at the same time they are demanding longer hours and more work.

Often unrecognized is the gradual eroding of wages. According to the Bureau of Labor Statistics, weekly wages adjusted for inflation rose every single decade between 1830 and 1970. Since then, wages first stagnated and then actually dropped.[17]

Today, most salaries are stagnant, and many people work more hours for the same amount of money or less. In truth it is because of inflation, which means the dollar today buys significantly less than the dollar of a few years ago

Why work fifty, sixty, seventy hours six days a week for someone else? Why not become a Wealth Rebel and invest this time and effort in your own business, something that you control and that builds equity for you and your family?

Yet the vast majority of people who are laid off will go right back into the job market hoping that, somehow, the next job will be different. And while the next job may indeed be different, there is no guarantee it will be any better than the last one. In fact, it may be worse.

> *If your success is not on your own terms, if it looks good to the world but does not feel good in your heart, it is not success at all.*
> —Anna Quindlen

According to Career Builder, "a full 77 percent [of employees surveyed] reported that they feel burnt out on their jobs."[18] TechLinks reports on job dissatisfaction, saying, "A recent Accenture study suggests that approximately 60 percent of today's workers and 50 percent of middle managers are unhappy in their current jobs and are willing to join the hunt."[19]

How many people do you know who really like getting up and commuting back and forth to work five days a week or more? How many of your friends really enjoy their jobs? How many of your friends with jobs feel truly secure about their future?

How about you? How do you really feel about your job?

BENEFITS OF BEING A WEALTH REBEL

What, exactly, is a Wealth Rebel? A Wealth Rebel is:
- A contrarian who thinks outside the box.
- An optimistic risk taker who blazes their own trail, making things happen because they see opportunities instead of obstacles.
- Someone who knows that self-employment is the real key to security and riches.

In other words, a Wealth Rebel is an entrepreneur, and entrepreneurs are Wealth Rebels.

The benefits of working for yourself add up in some surprising ways. Even if the idea is new to you, you can probably come up with several reasons it might be a good idea without much thought at all.

Here is a partial list of reasons to work for yourself to get you started:

1. **You get to be your own boss.** This is perhaps the biggest reason why people go into business for themselves. According to a recent study, the number-one reason for quitting a job is because of management.[20]

    Everyone has had a boss that they could not stand or was very hard to get along with. Going into business for yourself solves this problem.

2. **You will never again be passed over for advancement because of your gender, race, creed, or sexual orientation.** For women and minorities, self-employment offers a chance to wave goodbye to the glass and other ceilings, allowing you to fully utilize your strengths and talents regardless of your background.

3. **You will never have to watch your boss take credit for ideas you originated.** Supervisors are notorious for taking credit for underlings' ideas. If this has not yet happened to you, it probably will. And you have probably seen it happen to someone else. Self-employment solves this problem too.

4. **You will not have to cover for someone else's mistakes or be put in a position where you have to compromise your integrity.** As your own boss, you can choose who you want to work with and who you don't. Never again will you have to work beside stupid, lazy, ass-kissing morons. Corporate red tape will not tie your hands or be force you to follow the chain of command regardless of whether you feel it is right or not.

5. **You will never again be denied a promotion or a job because you did not have the right degree or attend the right college or university.** Many people get dead-ended on jobs or even fail to get hired at all because they do not have the "right" degree or graduated from the "wrong" college or university. When you own your own business, you are using your own skills regardless of how or where you acquired them[21]

English entrepreneur Sir Richard Branson, sometimes known simply as SRB, is a perfect example of a Wealth Rebel. Born in 1950, he is best known today for the Virgin brand he created, which included Virgin Records and Virgin Atlantic Airways.

He suffered from dyslexia as a child, and school was always difficult for him. By age fifteen, he had started two businesses—a Christmas tree farm and growing budgies (called parakeets by many). Both ventures failed and he left school the following year, moving to London.

In London at sixteen, he began to experience success by founding *Student* magazine. The next year he started his first charity, the Student Valley Centre.

It was not long before he began selling from the trunk of his car records he purchased at discounts, setting the stage for major changes in the way the music industry handled its pricing. It was during this period that he also started using the business name, Virgin.

In 1984, Branson founded Virgin Atlantic Airways, and he eventually sold Virgin Records to keep the airline afloat. The same year, he jumped into the then-young mobile phone industry with Virgin Mobile. By 2000 he had extended his airline business to Virgin Blue in Australia. The same year, he failed in a bid to run the United Kingdom's National Lottery.

> *The critical ingredient is getting off your butt and doing something. It's as simple as that. A lot of people have ideas, but there are few who decide to do something about them now. Not tomorrow. Not next week. But today. The true entrepreneur is doer, not just a dreamer.*
> —Nolan Bashnell, founder of Atari Computers & Chuck E. Cheese restaurant franchises

Today, Branson is recognized as one the of the world's richest men, with a financial worth of over five billion dollars. On October 12, 2006, he promised to donate at least three billion dollars over the next ten years to fight global warming.

Not bad for a school dropout!

WHY JOBS ARE NOT THE ANSWER

In a very real way, when you have a job you are actually selling or renting out yourself and your talents. Your employer is buying or renting your services and has a huge amount of control over how you spend your time as well as how much time you spend in exchange for your salary. This means, among other things, you can be fired from that job any time the employer wants.

Have you ever wondered why an employer wants two-weeks or more notice if you plan to quit, yet they can fire you without any warning whatsoever? Is that what you call security? This really is not any way to live your life, is it?

Fortunately, you have more options than you suspect.

When you work for yourself, no one can fire you! Owning your own business is not only the way to real wealth, it is the only way to create any sort of real job security.

Want more reasons why you should become a Wealth Rebel and start your own business? Consider these additional items:

1. **Higher income.** When you own your own business, there is no ceiling on your income—you are not limited to cost-of-living wage increases or performance reviews.

2. **Control.** You are in control when you own your own business. You call the shots, you make the decisions, and you grow it as big or keep it as small as you want. It is all up to you.

3. **Tax advantages.** There are considerable tax advantages to owning your own business, far greater than the withholding you are used to at a job. You can deduct your business expenses such as your automobile, meals, cell phone, office supplies, and travel.

4. **Flexible schedule and location.** You get to decide when and where to work when you own your own business.

5. **Building equity.** Owning your own business lets you build income and equity for yourself, not someone else. The equity in your business can often be sold or willed to your children. Try that with a job!

6. **Secure retirement.** It is much easier to secure your retirement when you own your own business

because you are in control of your income and your savings and because you are building equity.

FACTS ABOUT SELF-EMPLOYMENT

Let's look at some facts about self-employment:

1. A recently released study conducted by the U.S. Small Business Administration says, "The study finds that in 2001 small business-owning households were more than twice as likely as non-owning households to be high income earners and over eight times more likely to be high wealth households."[22]

2. According to the International Data Corporation, in 1999 there were about 18.8 million home businesses in existence, and that number grew to about 25 million in 2003. (Talk about short commutes!)[23]

3. Fifty-seven percent of small-business owners started or acquired their business with less than five thousand dollars, 25 percent required no money at all to start their own business, and only 19 percent used capital based on a personal loan.[24]

4. Although many people believe that 80 percent of businesses fail within five years, statistics from the U.S. Census Bureau reveal a different story. The Census Bureau reports that 76 percent of all small businesses operating in 1992 were still in business in 1996. In fact, only 17 percent of all small businesses that closed in 1997 were reported as bankruptcies or other failure. The rest that closed shut down because the business

was sold or incorporated or because the owner retired.[25]

5. There are an estimated 10.4 million privately held businesses in the U.S. where women hold 50 percent or more ownership in the business. That accounts for more than 40 percent of all businesses in the country.[26]

In other words, your chances of succeeding in a business of your own are good—very good, in fact.

IT'S ABOUT YOUR FREEDOM

Each one of the above solid reasons to become an entrepreneur and start your own business add up to one word:
Freedom!

Your freedom is what we are really talking about. Although the market will determine if your business will be hugely successful, you will have real freedom as a result of becoming an entrepreneur.

Some people call this creative freedom. In fact, creative freedom is one of the top reasons people start their own business. With all these very good reasons, why don't more people open their own businesses? In the next chapter we will look at some of the ideas and myths that keep people from becoming entrepreneurs.

CHAPTER 3

What's Wrong with What I'm Doing Now?

There is nothing so useless as doing efficiently that which should not be done at all.
Peter Drucker

What is wrong with what you are doing now? Good question—let's take a look. If you are like the average middle-income American:

•

- You are swimming in debt, with about a half dozen credit cards, each carrying an outstanding balance.
- You are barely able to make the minimum monthly payments on those credit cards.
- You are thinking about buying that next car, which you do about every two years.
- You have little or no money in the bank, and you are just one or two paychecks away from being broke.
- You have a home with a first mortgage, a second mortgage, and maybe an equity line of credit you use pretty freely.

- You are wondering what to do with your 401(k) plan but so far have not taken the time to understand it.
- You are wondering where you are going to borrow the money to send the kids to college.
- You have less (maybe way less) than fifty thousand dollars saved up for retirement.

Does any of this sound familiar to you? Do you identify with all or even some of the above points?

Let me ask you a question: If you continue doing what you are doing now, where will you really be financially in ten, fifteen, twenty, or thirty years? I am not asking about where you hope you will be or where you would like to be. Assuming you do not make a single change to your current situation, how will you actually end up?

The chances are if you keep doing what you are doing now, you will end up living like a king—a king in a third world country where the average citizen makes two dollars a day and has no running water or electricity.

Do you think this is not going to happen to you? According to the U.S. Census Bureau, the 2007 "poverty threshold" for a family of four was $21,203. The first question is, of course, how can a family of four live on just under $1,767 a month? Remember, that's before taxes.

Apparently it can be done because in August of 2007, the Census Bureau estimated that some thirty-seven million Americans live below that poverty line! That is a shocking number.

Perhaps even more startling is that we have 3.5 million homeless in this country, according to a 2007 study done by the National Law Center on Homelessness and Poverty.

Although the exact number is hard to pin down, more and more families are living paycheck to paycheck, just one step away from being homeless. How many paychecks are you away from serious financial difficulties?

How do we, the United States of America, produce thirty-seven million people below the poverty line? Do you for one minute think any one of these thirty-seven million people enjoy living in poverty? Do you think they had a plan?

It is safe to say, I think, that each of these people had a plan only in the sense they went along to get along. That means they had an unconscious plan and the notion that somehow their employer, their government, or someone else would take care of them. What went wrong?

The truth is, one way or another they became complacent. They thought all they had to do was to show up and someone would hand them a future. Many of them believed that just having a job, a place to live, and maybe a car meant they were living the America Dream. They thought that getting a decent job was all they needed to be successful in life.[27]

Make no mistake about it— many of the poor today have had, at one point

> *Take all the money you have in the world and add to that whatever you can borrow from friends and family members. Develop a good five-year business plan and stick to it. Invest 10 years of 14 to 16 hour days, six to seven days a week, giving your customers the highest levels of service and attention. Treat everyone on your staff like business partners. And always keep a close eye on your accounts receivable, your accounts payable, and your financial statements.*
> —Belinda Guadarrama, founder of GC Micro

> About 67 percent of Americans rely on their next paycheck to meet current living expenses, according to the 2007 online survey conducted for the American Payroll Association.

or another, a reasonably good job. These are the people who started the race. Somewhere along the line it is as if they were told to stop running and stood still. Standing still is not the way you win a race. If you are planning on a future with some comfort and security, you had better make some changes right now.

Sometimes change is forced on people. Belinda Guadarrama knew the mail-order business she worked for near San Francisco was in trouble, but she did not realize how much until she came to work one day only to find a notice on the door stating the business was closed.

"I was at a turning point in my life," she said. "I liked working in the computer field, so I could either start my own business doing that or look for a job in San Francisco. I decided to start my own company."

Belinda started GC Micro, a value-added software reseller, in 1986. Initially she applied for a five thousand-dollar bank loan but was almost laughed out of the bank. She left without even receiving a loan application.

With nothing more than sheer grit and determination, she sold her home. By the end of her first year, her new business claimed an income of $209,000. It took some time, but Belinda overcame the perception that a minority woman did not belong in the technology field or marketing to defense-related contractors.

Today, GC Micro is one of the country's most respected suppliers of hardware and software to both the defense and the aerospace industries.[28]

Reality Check

Here is a quick quiz to help you with a reality check:

- Who do you think makes more money, the employee of a company or the officers and owners?
- Who do you think will be better off financially, the guy who owns his home or the one who just rents?

- Who ends up with more money in the bank, the steady saver or the gambler?
- Who ends up creating wealth, the investor or the consumer-spender?
- Who do you think has more security in life, the person with money or the one living in poverty?
- Who ends up being able to help others, the person with a few extra bucks or the one who is always broke and looking for a handout?
- Who do think is more relaxed and happy, the person with a sizable nest egg, or the person who is living paycheck to paycheck, always trying to make ends meet?

The answers are obvious, aren't they? So is the fact that it is time for you to make a change. Take a moment and think about it— have you fallen into a life-rut? You know what a rut is, don't you? It is a grave with the ends kicked out.

Are you in a rut? Now, answer these questions:

- What, exactly, are you doing about your future and your retirement?
- What, exactly, are you doing to assure you and your family will have what you need and be able to live the way you want to live five, ten, or twenty years from now?

Answer these questions honestly, knowing that if you are typical or even close to it, the truth is you are not doing as much as you need to and nor are you doing nearly as much as you could be doing.

Oh, you may have a steady job with predictable pay increases and a 401(k) plan. If you are lucky, you have some health coverage and are buying your own home. You may even be the exception to the rule and have a thousand or two in savings. You might even have the recommended three-to-six-months' living expenses saved. But is it enough? Are you leading the life today you truly want to lead? Do you know if you are prepared or preparing adequately for the future? Are you willing to actually look at your situation?

MISCONCEPTIONS OF YOUR CURRENT LIFE PLAN

Whether or not you are aware of it, you do have a life plan. That is, you are set on a course. It is a direction that unless you consciously make a change, governs your life today and your life in the future.

The trouble is most people are not aware of the life plan they have set up or adopted for themselves. Instead they are swept up in the tide of following the norm without ever really taking time to examine it. That path, unless we consciously change it, is a product of our society and not of our own design, desire, and dreams.

For example, society tells us many things, including these seven basic myths:

1. To be successful you need to get a college education.
2. The more education you get, the more money you will earn.
3. A good-paying job is your ticket to security in the future.
4. Owning your own home guarantees security.
5. The stock market is a great way to grow your money and get rich.
6. It is okay to carry a certain amount of credit card debt—credit card debt is a great way to purchase stuff.
7. Social Security will provide adequately for your retirement.

Each of these seven myths shapes many of the decisions you make about your life. These decisions make up your life plan. Make no mistake about it—your life plan will determine your future even if you are unconscious of it.

The first step is to take a close look at each of these myths and how they are impacting your life right now. Let's look at each:

1. **To be successful you need to get a college education.**
2. **The higher the degree, the more money you will earn.**

   As we show in the next chapter in more detail, education, or the lack thereof, is no real predictor of success. A college or graduate degree may make it easier to get certain jobs, but as you will learn, jobs are not the answer to solving the wealth puzzle.

3. **A good-paying job is your ticket to security in the future.**

   This is far from the truth. A job, even a good one with benefits and a 401(k) plan or other pension is, these days, no guarantee of security. There is simply too much going on in the economy, from outsourcing to global competition, to make any job a path to security.

4. **Owning your own home guarantees security.**

   I am all in favor of owning real estate, but owning your own home does not guarantee your future. Properly handled, the equity in your home, if you own one, may be used to fund your own business, but given the up-and-down nature of the real estate market, it makes no sense to put all your security eggs into only the home-owing basket.

5. **The stock market is a great way to grow your money and get rich.**

   If you paid any attention to the first chapter, you already know this is not true. If you have a 401(k) plan, now is the time to carefully examine what it is actually doing for you. Look carefully at the statements you have received, and if you do not have them all, get the company to send them to you again. Notice how much of your paycheck is going in, how much you are being charged in fees, and, most importantly, how much or how little the money you have contributed has grown.

   If your employer is matching your contributions, you may be doing okay at the moment, but if you are the sole contributor the chances are there has not been much gain. Either way, find out exactly what is happening. It may be that the money in your 401(k) plan can be put to better use.

6. **It is okay to carry a certain amount of credit card debt—credit card debt is a great way to purchase stuff.**

   This societal myth is truly deadly. We are constantly surrounded with messages that assure us we will be happy if only we buy more stuff on credit. The problem with credit card debt is twofold:

   - It is unsecured—that is, unlike real estate or a car loan, there is nothing the lender can take in return if for some reason you are unable to pay, which is one reason the rates are so high. With a secured loan, if you get into trouble you have the option of selling secured assets to satisfy the loan.

With credit card debt your options are limited and expensive.

- If you do not pay each card off in full every month, the interest and fees can eat you alive. The average credit card debt of the typical American ranges from $2,000 to $7,000, depending on who you listen to.[29] If we split the difference and say you owe $5,000 on credit cards, with a typical rate of 19 percent you can make payments of $461 a month, incur no additional charges, and be out of debt in twelve months. If you continue to charge at a rate of $275 a month but make minimum payments of $375, you will literally never get out of debt. On the other hand, if you paid the balance right now, you would save $579 in interest.

You can determine exactly how much your credit card debt is costing you at any number of Web sites. One good source is www.bankrate.com, or you can call your credit card companies and ask them. However you do it, find out exactly how much you owe and how exactly much it is costing you. Then explore your options.

7. **Social Security will provide for you.**
   All discussion of an upcoming crisis in Social Security aside, the chances are you do not know how much you will be entitled to, but you can find out. Just go to http://www.ssa.gov/ and click on *Calculate Your Benefits*. You will have to enter the amounts you have earned and expect to earn, but you will get a ballpark figure of your future benefits. Most people discover that if Social Security pays at all, it will pay way less than they need for a reasonable, let alone comfortable,

retirement. You cannot rely solely on Social Security to provide your total retirement needs. You must find a better way.

Do you see how you have been misled? Even if you have not fallen for all of these myths, chances are you have fallen for at least one and probably more.

This does not mean all is lost—far from it. But you need to let go of these myths and figure out exactly where you are to make an effective change.

IT DOES NOT WORK ANYMORE

It may help to understand that each one of these myths was more or less true at one time in the past, which is why they are so pervasive today. Almost all the advertising we are inundated with all day, every day tends to promote and/or support these myths. Chances are your parents taught you these myths without even realizing it. You were certainly led to believe many of these myths at school. Most of the books, magazines, and newspapers you read support these myths with both their content and their advertising. If you have a typical job, most of your co-workers have bought into these myths. Unfortunately, many of your friends likely also hold these views.

In fact, these myths govern your life plan so thoroughly that they are really hard to see. It is almost as if we have filters that prevent us from understanding the truth.

This is why it can be so difficult, at least at first, to even think about making a change.

LAW OF PHYSICS

Sir Isaac Newton stated, "Every object persists in its state of rest or uniform motion in a straight line unless it is compelled to change its state by forces impressed on it." To phrase it another way, objects in motion tend to stay in motion, while objects at rest tend to stay at rest. And so it is with us. Once we are set on a path we tend to stay on that path unless something knocks us off.

Job loss, illness, or other major difficulties are the typical things that get people to change what they are doing, but you do not have to wait for a major problem. Fortunately, you have the ability to make a change simply because you decide to.

Since the key to true security and wealth is starting your own business, which is what you need to decide to do and the sooner the better. Of course, like any major change, there are some barriers.

CHAPTER 4

WHY NOT TRY?

How am I going to live today in order to create the tomorrow I'm committed to?
Tony Robbins

It is easy to say, "I want to be rich." It is much harder to actually take the steps to create the financial freedom you want and deserve. It is tempting, when looking at all that is required to start your own business—and make no mistake about it, there is a lot that needs to be done—to quit even before you get started, saying in one way or another, "Why try?"

If you have a decent job with some benefits, it seems easier to just stay where you are. One of the reasons people tend to think this way is because they are unclear about the real "whys" of making a major change.

IT'S NOT ABOUT THE MONE

Building wealth by starting your own business really isn't about the money you can earn. We all know that money won't buy happiness, love, or respect. Happiness,

> *The person who makes a success of living is the one who see his goal steadily and aims for it unswervingly. That is dedication.*
> —Cecil B. DeMille

love, and respect are inside jobs earned by our view of ourselves and the results of the actions we take.

When you think about it, money is only a carrier of value and a medium of exchange.

Most people do not want money so much as they want what having money gives them. People want the feeling of freedom, the security, the fun, and the ability to be generous that having money helps them achieve.

At least for most people, focusing on the money itself simply does not work when it comes to building wealth. Life is, after all, about much more than money. We want a combination of security and freedom so we are free to pursue our passions, spend time with the people we love, and generally live a life of expansion rather than one of contraction.

In our society the truth is that wealth gives people the opportunity to expand and live life to the fullest—poverty or just getting by contracts us and narrows our view of ourselves. Whether you call it low income or poverty, lack of ample money limits our options.

MONEY GIVES YOU MORE OPTIONS

Having the kind of money you can only earn or create from your own business means having many more options and much more freedom. One way to define real freedom is *the ability to go where you want, with whom you want, and when you want.* It takes money to do this. In other words, money creates options and choices.

SECURITY

Security is something everyone longs for. The desire for safety is part of our makeup. One good definition of security is *freedom from anxiety or fear.* Generally that means, at a minimum:

- Enough good food to eat.
- A home to shelter us and our family.

- Good health, which also means good healthcare.
- Safety and a sense of safety.
- Security for our old age, including healthcare and living conditions.
- People who love and support us.
- The ability to help others.
- The desire to help change our world for the better.
- Leaving a legacy for our family and/or our community.
- Having enough possessions to make life easier.

Every single person, no matter how much money they have or do not have, needs each of the above items to have a real sense of safety and security. They need them not just for now but also for their whole lives. People know, even if they try to avoid thinking about it, that they will need these things when they retire. Having enough money to fund both the lifestyle they want today and the lifestyle they want in their retirement creates a sense of security.

But security means more than simply taking care of ourselves. It also means the ability to take care of others, including our family.

HEALTH

Your health and the health of your family is one of the most obvious examples of how money creates more options. Let me tell you the story of my Aunt Christina.

I watched as this wonderful woman battled breast cancer for ten years. She was a hard worker and made many sacrifices in her life, but because she did not have much money, she was limited as to the medical care and medications she could buy. She had health insurance through her work, but it did not cover the experimental or

> *I believe a little bit of success lies in everyone! Will you be the one to deny that? Or rather will you be the one who chooses to be guided by it? I hope you choose, as I have to do the latter!*
> —Josh S. Hinds

alternative treatments that might have helped, and in the end she lost her battle with cancer.

Contrast this with Tour de France multi-time winner Lance Armstrong. When his cancer was first diagnosed, he was told it was a Stage 3 cancer and he had about a 50 percent chance of recovery. When he did recover, one doctor said his chances for survival had actually been closer to 3 percent.

Armstrong had money and some fame going for him when he learned he had cancer. Although the details of his treatment and cure are vague, one thing is certain—his money gave him access to more treatment options than my Aunt Christina. It is also worth noting that Armstrong is a risk taker—he has a winning attitude. The combination of more treatment options plus his attitude undoubtedly contributed to his healing.

It may not be fair, but having money simply gives you many more choices and options, like better health insurance, gym memberships, and the ability to pay for alternative treatments and other treatments that simply are not covered by insurance. Under more health options we could also include real time off work and less stress. Having your own business and the wealth it creates can help give you and your family the options you need and deserve.

EDUCATION

Another area in which having the money your own business can generate creates significant options is education—for your children, your grandchildren, and even for you. Some of these advantages are fairly obvious. Although you do not need an advanced degree to successfully start your own business, options in education are truly valuable.

For example, would your children benefit from private school? Many parents want this option for their kids but simply cannot afford the requisite ten thousand dollars or more per child per year. Or maybe you would like the freedom to home school your kids. Having your own business can make this possible.

Of course, you may want to send your children to a really good college or university. As the costs of higher education increase, the number of people who can afford to attend decreases. Your personal solution is to have more money so you can pay the higher fees, and for most that means having their own business.

Maybe you or your spouse has always wanted to formally study art, playwriting, or music. Your own business can generate both the time and the money to allow you to do so.

Needless to say, education is not limited to school. Perhaps you would like to give your child or grandchild music lessons or voice lessons or send them to an expensive but effective soccer camp.

Then there are the options of travel for you and your family that having money can create, such as traveling to a foreign country, to learn the culture and the language. Having money makes all of this possible.

HELPING OTHERS

Helping others is another area where having financial resources makes a huge difference. Some people want to help their elderly parents, and others want to give generously to a church or charities or want to set up foundations that promote a particular cause. Look at what, for example, Bill Gates and Warren Buffet have been able to accomplish with their wealth.

The Bill & Melinda Gates Foundation has committed more than 7.8 billion dollars to date to support global health efforts.[30] Buffet set up a program allowing stockholders to designate their favorite charities for donations and created literally hundreds of billions of dollars for helping people all over the planet.

What would you do for others if you had the money to do it? Give some serious thought to this question, knowing that the key is starting your own business.

CONSIDER THE ALTERNATIVES

When you find yourself wondering if you should try to start your own business, consider the alternatives. It has been said many times: *if you keep doing what you're doing, you'll keep getting what you've got.*

> *Desire is the starting point of all achievement; not a hope, not a wish, but a keen pulsating desire, which transcends everything.*
> —Napoleon Hill

It may be worse than that! If you keep doing what you are doing and you lose your job, you will not even get to keep what you have.

Where do you really want to be next year, in five years, in ten years? Do you want to be doing what you are doing now, or is that a path to self-destruction, full of the risks of job loss and a poverty stricken retirement? What, exactly, is your life plan?

Ultimately, you are the only one who can take care of yourself and your family—no one else is going to do it for you. Government programs, if they exist, will not provide enough. You do not want to saddle your kids with responsibility for you—it truly is up to you.

If your current plan does not include self-employment and entrepreneurship, it is bound to fail. It is only a matter of when, not if.

What if you do not try? Think about what your life will look like when you are reflecting on your life from your sixties or seventies. What kind of excuses or stories will you tell your grandkids? The world is full of people living their lives with regret, but few get to say that they were able to live their dream once in their life.

When you are sixty-five, at the end of your working career, and corporate America has put you out to pasture, you will end up where you started—a few dollars in the bank and a life of memories. Without ownership you have no equity and no stake in the game. You were used by the corporation, discarded, and replaced by a younger (outsourced) employee, which starts the cycle over. So ask yourself, is this my financial future?

CHAPTER 5

Poor Excuses

Whether you think that you can, or that you can't, you are usually right.
Henry Ford

How many times have you been driving on a trip and the traffic comes to a complete stop because the road is blocked? What do you do? Do you turn around and go home, or do you look for a way around? You cannot let the little day-to-day roadblocks force you to retreat and go home in defeat.

Since true wealth and real freedom come from self-employment, it is only fair to point out that you will face some roadblocks to setting up your own business. After all, if there were not some problems and distractions, everyone would be an entrepreneur. The obstacles, however, are probably not what you expect.

It's All In Your Head

The first and biggest obstacle before you is you. That's right, you heard me correctly—it's you! You are the one most likely to get in your own way when it comes to becoming a successful entrepreneur. Before you reject this statement, below are some typical excuses people give for not going into business for themselves:

1. I have a family to take care of.
2. I don't have any (or not enough) time.
3. I don't have any (or not enough) money.
4. I don't have the right experience.
5. I don't have the right education.
6. I'm too old (or too young) to start my own business.
7. I'm afraid to make a mistake.
8. I'm afraid to fail.

Do any of these excuses sound familiar? It is this kind of thinking about yourself and your situation that is most likely to stop you from starting your own business. Let's look at these excuses one at a time and understand what the real truth is.

I HAVE A FAMILY TO TAKE CARE OF.

Good. Your first responsibility should be to your family. As much as this objection makes sense on the surface, playing it safe usually leads to a life of what-ifs, what-could-have-beens, and lost dreams.

But what if you knew that by becoming an entrepreneur you would be able to take better care of your family than you are able to right now? What if you saw that by starting your own business you were actually setting a positive example for your children? If you knew these things were true, how would that make you feel about owning and building your own business?

I DON'T HAVE ANY (OR NOT ENOUGH) TIME.

How is it that certain people are able to accomplish so much in just one day while others are barely able to get anything done by

> *Footprints on the sands of time are not made by sitting down.*
> —*unknown*

the end of the week? Believing you do not have enough time to start your own business is actually a myth.

Everyone has 168 hours each and every week. Assuming you are working a job that is roughly 40 hours a week, that leaves you with 128 hours. Of course, you have to sleep and spend time with your family. Sleeping takes about 56 hours a week, which leaves a bit over 10 hours every day or 72 hours each week for your discretionary use.

Some percentage of those 72 hours a week can be spent on creating your own business. Exactly how much will depend on your situation, but it can be done. You could, for example, watch less TV or hire someone to do the yard work—maybe even one of your own kids.

Trust me, once you realize what an advantage it is to start your own business, you will make the time! And you will find that you do have enough time—more than enough, in fact.

> *Happiness is not in the mere possession of money; it lies in the joy of achievement, in the thrill of creative effort.*
> —Franklin Roosevelt

I DON'T HAVE ANY (OR NOT ENOUGH) MONEY.

Would it surprise you to know that many businesses can be started with little or no money? It's true. As we said in chapter 2, 57 percent of small-business owners started or acquired their business with less than five thousand dollars. Twenty-five percent required no capital at all, and only 19 percent used money raised with a personal loan or with credit cards. Keep these facts in mind.[31]

For example, five years ago one of my clients, Leana, realized she could use her credentials and skills as a registered nutritionist and make money by putting together menus for nursing homes. She started her new business, which she called Long Term Care Nutrition, out of her home with an investment of less than five hundred dollars. Today she has a nice, six-figure income and came to me to learn how to maximize her money.

Or take my friend Larry—he has been involved in starting more than one company without ever having to use any of his own money. The first venture was Conceptions Unlimited Ltd., which he formed in 1978 with a partner. The purpose was to create software systems for manufacturing and construction companies using the Wang Laboratories Mini Computers. By the end of its first year, CUL had four employees and probably did a couple hundred thousand dollars of business. The business continued to grow slowly until, in the mid 1980s, the entire business was threatened by the desktop computer. CUL could not compete price-wise, and nor did they have the technical expertise to deal with desktops, but they were able to carve out a niche providing new applications to various markets as a service bureau business.

> *Always bear in mind that your own resolution to succeed is more important than any other one thing.*
> —Abraham Lincoln

In 1991, Conceptions Unlimited Ltd. had forty-five employees and was doing about 3.5 million dollars as a company. Although the company was successful, growth was slow because the business was financed from within.

In 1992, Larry founded Retailvision to distribute special-interest consumer magazines to retail outlets. Not content to bootstrap this company and grow slowly, Larry picked a partner from within the publishing business who had a keen interest in financing the start-up and building the business quickly.

The first thing Larry did was hire five marketing people to launch the services once the initial software system was ready to go. The company grew rapidly and became a standard in the publishing industry. Retailvision bought Conceptions Unlimited Ltd. in 1999.

When he left the company in 2000, it had eighty-five employees and was doing about fifty-five million dollars per year with a fifteen thousand-square foot office and distribution centers in Pittsburg, Chicago, and Bakersfield, California. It is still the leader in retail distribution for special-interest consumer magazines.

These people, by just getting up and going, were able to start and run successful businesses with little or no initial capital.

I DON'T HAVE THE RIGHT EXPERIENCE.

This is one of those statements that if you look at honestly really does not make much sense. When it comes to starting or purchasing a business, you will draw on your past experiences and your passions. Do you think Bill Gates knew how to run a computer company when he started Microsoft? Or did Richard Branson think he needed years of experience in order to start Virgin Records?

Turn this statement around and ask yourself what sorts of experience you actually do have. Whatever your current job, you probably know much more than your job title indicates.

Make a list of your other life experiences, such as managing a household, keeping a car repaired, and keeping track of financial issues like purchasing and working within a budget. The list of what you know and what you have actually done will likely turn out much longer and more extensive than you first thought, and it will go a long way toward convincing you that you do have the experience you need to start your own business.

> *Small opportunities are often the beginning of great enterprises.*
> —Demosthenes

Brian Scudamore is an outstanding example of someone who started a business with no experience and little money. He left high school in 1989 with seven hundred dollars and an old, beat-up truck to start his own junk removal company. Three summers later, he knew he had a success on his hands. Hiring student drivers and investing in a few more trucks, he named his service, "1-800-GOT-JUNK?" Today, his is the largest junk removal company in the country, with franchises across North America.

Scudamore was a risk taker with a clear dream. "With a vision of creating the FedEx of junk removal," says Scudamore, "I dropped out of university with just one year left to become a fulltime junkman! Yes, my father, a liver-transplant surgeon, was not impressed to say the least." He chuckles, "He is onside now."

Scudamore hired a buddy in the first week. "I always believed in hiring people versus using contractors or consultants. I felt that if I wasn't willing to make the investment then I was questioning my own faith in the business."

But he is also more than willing to share both the risk and the success, which is why he chose franchising as a model for growth. "It's the ultimate leverage model. People pay you a fee up front to help them grow." He sees franchising as the only way to keep control, whereas going public and issuing stock puts the control in other people's hands.

> *Too many people overvalue what they are not and undervalue what they are.*
> —Malcolm Forbes

He has managed to retain 100 percent ownership of his company and bootstrapped the business solely out of cash flow.

By 2004, Scudamore was on track to do about 34 million dollars-worth of business, and he anticipates 100 million dollars with at least 250 franchise partners by Dec 31, 2006. He says confidently, "We will get there."[32]

The truth is that starting and running your own business is a lot like starting a new job. You were hired because you had certain skills, but much of a new job involves learning new things and new ways of working. Just as it takes a while to get comfortable in a new job, it will take a while for you to get comfortable with running your own business. But remember—with your own business, you are building something solid for you and your family, not creating wealth for someone else.

I DON'T HAVE THE RIGHT EDUCATION

The truth is there is no specific education needed to become a successful entrepreneur. The common misconception is that you need a college degree in order to own and run a successful business. Put it another way—you may think you are just not smart enough to run a business unless you prove it by getting a college degree. That is an absolute lie. Consider the list of thirty-seven billionaires who do not have college degrees. Each one of them is on Forbes Magazine's 2005 400 List, which is a list of the wealthiest people in America.

Bill Gates may be the most obvious example of huge success with no college degree. Born in Seattle, Washington, in 1955, he was an outstanding student, excelling in science and math. He took to computers as soon as his school purchased a terminal and a block of time on a General Electric mainframe.

He entered Harvard in 1973. In his junior year, he left to devote his time to Microsoft, the company he founded in 1975.

The rest is history. Without a college degree, Gates has become not just the wealthiest man in the world but one of the most generous, contributing billions through the Bill & Melinda Gates Foundation.[33]

Do not let anyone tell you that you are not smart enough to run a business just because you do not have college degree.[34]

Billionaires who do not have a college degree:

Bill Gates
Paul Allen
Richard Branson
Larry Ellison
Richard M. Schulze
Steven Jobs
Sheldon Adelson
Dan L. Duncan
Jack C. Taylor
Micky Arison
David Geffen
David Howard Murdock
James Sorenson
Ronald Burkle
David Green
Daniel Abraham
William J. Pulte
Kenneth Hendricks
James Jannard
James M. Moran
Malcolm Glazer
Phillip Ruffin
Theodore Waitt
Pincus Green
William Morean
Stephen J. Bisciotti
Truett Cathy

I'M TOO OLD (OR TOO YOUNG) TO START MY OWN BUSINESS

There is no right age for starting your own business. To put it another way, successfull businesses have been started by people of all ages. You may be sixteen or eighty-six, but if you have a great idea and a burning desire to turn it into a successful business, go for it—do not let anyone stop you.

You have only to know the story of Harland David Sanders, known to most as Colonel Sanders of Kentucky Fried Chicken, to recognize age simply does not matter.

> *Live your life and forget your age.*
> —Norman Vincent Peale

Sanders started cooking for his family when he was six years old and his father died. As a teenager he held many jobs. By the time he was forty, he owned his own service station and started cooking for folks in his home, which was attached to the station.

His cooking grew in popularity, and he moved to a motel that had a restaurant that seated almost one hundred fifty people. He served as chef and over the next nine years perfected his secret recipe which included the same "eleven herbs and spices" used today.

In 1952, at the age of sixty-two, he began franchising his recipe by traveling from restaurant to restaurant and cooking up batches of chicken. When a restaurant wanted to feature his chicken, he created, with only a handshake, an agreement that the restaurant would pay him a nickel for every serving of his chicken they sold. Eventually, he turned his franchise into the fast food chain we see literally around the world.[35]

At the other end of the age scale is Stephen J. Bisciotti, who is best known as the second-youngest NFL owner. He started Aerotek, a service company designed to provide engineers for the aerospace industry, when he was twenty-three. Aerotek grew to become the third-largest recruiting firm in the

> *Strong people make as many mistakes as weak people. The difference is that strong people admit their mistakes, laugh at them, and learn from them. That is how they become strong.*
> —Richard Needham

U.S. and the sixth largest in the world. Along the way, the name of the company changed to the Allegis Group.

Bisciotti is now a member of Forbes Richest 400, where, in 2006, his wealth was estimated at 960 million dollars and rising.[36]

I'M AFRAID TO MAKE A MISTAKE

You are finally beginning to identify the main reason for not becoming an entrepreneur—your fear.

Now, take a closer look at the statement, "I'm afraid to make a mistake." Is that really true? Are you really afraid of *any* mistake you might make? Chances are something happened to you this week that could be called a mistake or an error. We all make mistakes and often. Usually, however, the consequences are not that bad. In fact, if we are willing, those mistakes become learning experiences. Remember, the people who do not make mistakes are the ones who never try anything.

Did you know that most space shuttles are off course[37] at certain times during their flights and have to adjust accordingly? The same is also common among commercial airliners flying from coast to coast. The reason the shuttle reaches the moon and your jet brings you to your destination is because they both make constant, small course corrections along the way. You automatically do the same thing when you are driving.

Mistakes are not the problem—we only get into trouble if we fail to make the correction.

WHAT IF I FAIL

Once again, you are getting close to the core of what prevents you from becoming an entrepreneur. For the moment, however, let's compare this statement with what is at risk with a job. In a traditional job, you can be fired, your income is predetermined

> *A failure is a man who has blundered but is not capable of cashing in on the experience.*
> —Elbert Hubbard

and limited by your employer, and you have no ownership in the company you work for.

Of course there are risks in starting your own business, but there are equal and perhaps even greater risks in not becoming an entrepreneur or Wealth Rebel.

Remember, building your own business is the only true way to establish real wealth and attain the security wealth can bring you.

YOUR FEAR IS THE REAL BARRIER

As you have probably begun to suspect, fear is what prevents most people from starting their own business. Fear results in self-limiting thoughts and excuses. Fear has been defined as False Emotions Appearing Real. When fears surface, and they will, take a closer look at their source or reason—oftentimes you will discover that your fears are unfounded.

To become successful with your own business, you have to overcome your self-doubt, fear-based thinking, and pessimism. Do not worry, it can be done. Lots of people have turned their thinking around, and you can too. We will show you how.

> *You gain strength, courage, and confidence by every experience in which you really stop to look fear in the face. You must do the thing which you think you cannot do.*
> —Eleanor Roosevelt

Start by remembering the dreams you had as you were growing up. Another way to do this is to ask yourself what you were doing just before you realized you had to work for a living. We will take a closer look at this in the next chapter.

There is nothing I hate seeing more than someone killing their own dream. I call it *dreamicide*. It is self-sabotaging behavior. However it happens, you did not do it by yourself—part of the problem are behaviors and patterns of thinking that have been programmed into us since we were infants. The educational system reinforces dream-killing ideas by subtly and not so subtly insisting that everyone prepare for a job. Well-meaning friends and family, who have bought into these same negative ideas, often reinforce the notion that our dreams are meant to be left behind. Ask yourself, who do you know that gave up their dream or passion for a "secure job"? An example would be a young man who is passionate about art and yet is advised to pick a major that will pay well as opposed to one that embodies his dream.

There is another way. To overcome your fears, you have to change your thinking and your behavior. The only way to do that is one step at a time. First, you want to identify the origin of your fear. Does your fear have an irrational source such as a mystery novel or horror film? Was it implanted by your parents when you were a child or by a negative life experience? For example, are you afraid of riding a horse because you were thrown off one as child? In order to overcome fear, you must begin to break it down to its basic source. Once you have found the source, the next step is to start challenging it. Begin by trying an endeavor or experience that you never imagined you could. Do the thing you fear the most and the death of fear is certain. With enough practice, your new way of thinking and being will become a habit and a real part of you.

All you have to do right now is decide you are willing to make the necessary changes.

WATCH OUT FOR THE DREAM KILLERS

Once you have decided to change your thoughts to supporting the idea of becoming an entrepreneur, you cannot allow anyone to detour you from your dreams of creating wealth. You will probably notice that some of the people around you will not be supportive of your desire to start your own business. Some will tell you outright lies in order to discourage you from striking out on your own.

Well-meaning but misinformed people like your parents, brothers, sisters, friends, spouse, neighbors, and acquaintances do not realize they are passing along untruths. For example, you will hear people say things like, "You can't run a business because you have no experience, no money, no training, no education, etc." They simply repeat false information that has been passed on from unreliable sources, never questioning it to see whether it is true or not.

Then there are the "Wendy Whiners" of the world. These are the people who always have to cast a negative light on other people's dreams because of jealousy, dissatisfaction with their own lives, or a number of other reasons related to their own personal fears and agendas.

Whatever the source, these naysayers are the most insidious threat to a budding Wealth Rebel because they can get to you psychologically. Once their comments are planted in your mind, they will throw doubt on everything you are trying to achieve. Do not let them kill your dream!

Here are three steps to fighting the naysayers in your life:

1. **Consider the source.** Start by asking yourself about the person who is making the negative comment. Is there any real reason to believe they know what they are talking about? Are they, for example, a successful entrepreneur? Is this a person who has accomplished something in the business world?

   Most of the time you will realize the person in question has no personal experience on which to base their negative comments. You can safely ignore what they say.

2. **Is the information reliable?** What is the source of the information? If the naysayer is passing on information from a third party, ask yourself how

the naysayer got the information. Is it reliable or is it just hearsay? Rumors, myths, and outright lies have ruined many a path to creating wealth. You can safely ignore these comments too.

3. **Verification.** Research the information. If it seems reliable, ask the same sorts of questions about the third party. Who is the third party? Are they a successful entrepreneur or businessperson? If by some chance it turns out the party quoted is a successful entrepreneur, follow up to make sure what is being passed along is accurate. You might even want to contact the third party yourself.

   You do not want to ignore information that can help you avoid mistakes, but you must make sure it comes from a person who is qualified to comment.

Be extra careful when the naysayer is truly close to you. Many times our closest family members are real culprits, making some of the most psychologically damaging statements. Often they are projecting their own fears onto you and your visions.

We are extra vulnerable here because in our hearts and minds we want the people closest to us to be proud of us, to support our endeavors, and to share in our dreams. We seek their approval. This is especially true when that person is a parent, sibling, or spouse. The closer the individual, the more dangerous they can be.

Your spouse can be your greatest asset and support, or they can be your worst enemy if they have a negative attitude. If a spouse cannot or will not let go of their own fears, you may come to a point where you have to make a decision between your spouse and your real purpose in life.

DREAM KILLERS ARE RISK ADVERSE

Most dream killers are not even aware of what they are doing. They do not set out to sabotage you and nor do they want you to fail. They are simply more adverse to risk than you are. They turn their own fears into negative commentary on your dreams.

What they are really saying is that they do not want to take any risk—they are too afraid to start a business or consider leaving a job. Naysayers are usually telling you a whole lot more about themselves than about what is really true.

> *You see things; and you say, "Why?" But I dream things that never were; and I say, "Why not?"*
> —George Bernard Shaw

If it is your parents that are doing the nay-saying, remember they are older and as a result have a whole different set of experiences than you do. Because of this they are in a different stage of life.

Also keep in mind that they have not done the research you have done, and they have not spoken to the people you have.

The best way to deal with this kind of naysayer when you encounter them is to just thank them for their advice and let them know that you will take it into consideration. Do not argue with them, as it will only get both of you upset and will not accomplish anything. Understand where they are coming from. They are concerned for you but they do not know as much as you do about your idea or your business. They are acting out of fear, and you are acting out of knowledge and opportunism.

What kind of support do you suppose Bill Gates had when he started Microsoft? How about Richard Branson who founded, among other things, Virgin Airlines, or Oprah Winfrey, Henry Ford, Mark Cuban, Donald Trump, Michael Dell, Rich Devos, Martha Stewart, JP Morgan, Dave Thomas, Colonel Sanders, Thomas Edison, Emeril Lagasse, Anthony Robbins, and others? Undoubtedly there were naysayers along the line for each of these people, but if you read their biographies, you will discover that they did not allow people around them to negatively influence them or deter them from following their dream.

AVOID MR. AND MS. NEGATIVITY

A different type of danger to your dream is "Mr. or Ms. Negativity." You know the type. Everything that seems to come out of their mouth is negative. They never have anything good to say, and they are miserable as a result. Unfortunately, they love trying to spread their misery and small thinking around.

They are easy to identify because they are always saying things like:

> *Winning is a habit. Unfortunately, so is losing.*
> —Vince Lombardi

- "That won't work."
- "You can't do that."
- "You will only end up failing and back where you started."
- "What makes you think you can start and run a business?"
- "You can't make any money at that."
- "What do you know about (fill in the blank)?"

When you find yourself with this kind of person, run! Get as far away from them as you can as quickly as humanly possible. Their condition is highly contagious and will kill your dream before you even get started.

In fact, we suggest making a habit of finding those people who are on the opposite end of the spectrum. You can call them, "Mr. or Ms. Positive." Surround yourself with positive folks and let their attitudes rub off on you. Being a positive person is a sure sign of future success.

Obviously we are not suggesting that you should not listen to anyone—not at all. What we are saying is you want to surround yourself with people who are willing and qualified to support your dream. Seek out successful entrepreneurs. Find others who are pursuing their dreams. You will be glad you did.

Now that you understand the path to wealth lies in starting a business and know how to avoid some of the barriers to starting your own business, the next question is, how do you actually start?

CHAPTER 6

DREAM LIKE A CHILD—FIND YOUR PASSION

Chase your passion, not your pension.
Denis Waitley

It may seem odd, but the place to start planning your future business is in your dreams. Yes, now is the time to get in touch with the dreams and passions you either left behind or have been ignoring because you did not think they were practical.

The reason you need to discover or rediscover your passion is that it takes dedication fueled by excitement and enthusiasm to generate the sustained energy you will need to start and succeed in your own business. Enthusiasm and excitement is the stuff dreams are made of.

TAKE TIME TO DREAM

Once in a while someone will know, without much thought, exactly the kind of business they want to start. But this is rare. Also rare are the people who are more interested in the mechanics of business than in the business itself—these folks can be happy with almost any type of business they can make run well.

> *Dreams are extremely important. You can't do it unless you imagine it.*
> —George Lucas

Most people, however, do better when they can combine their passions with their business interests, and that takes dreaming. Getting in touch with your dream usually takes some serious time and self-investigation.

It was not always this way. When we were kids we never hesitated to express our dreams. Practicality and the real world never entered our minds when we first said we wanted to be a fireman, a ballerina, a writer, or a professional ballplayer.

As we grew into adulthood, however, we found we were often encouraged to give up our dreams. Our parents may have said things like, "You can't be an astronaut," "Artists can't make a living," "You're not tall enough to play basketball," "Girls can't be congressmen," etc. Gradually, we learned first not to speak about our dreams and then later to suppress them altogether.

Now is the time to begin dreaming all over again. Make an agreement with yourself that you will ignore any nay-saying voice, either internal or external; suggesting that whatever you discover is not practical or possible. Do not let logic get in the way.

For within even that seemingly impossible dream is information that, if you allow it to develop, will lead you to the perfect self-employment opportunity. Go ahead and dream— later we will show you how to access the hidden information.

Do not be surprised if the whole dreaming process takes several days, weeks, or even months. It is very important that you do not rush this process. Be patient with yourself and know that it will all start to become clear. Know too that all this work is more than worth the time you spend on it. After all, you are getting ready to start your own business.

You need to have one place where you can collect all the information you generate about starting your own business. I suggest a notebook, file folder, or computer folder to help you keep this information organized. This way you will know exactly where to go when you want to refer to something.

> *The key to happiness is having dreams. The key to success is making your dreams come true.*
> —Anonymous

STARTING A DREAMING LIST

A good way to discover what your dreams really are is to start making lists. Dream lists are not to-do lists. A to-do list acts as a discipline, giving you a sense of structure. Dream lists are designed to free up your thoughts and feelings. On a dream list you are allowed to put down anything you want, with no restrictions whatsoever. You are only limited by your imagination.

By the way, when you are making your dream list, keep in mind that it does not have to be linear. Some people find that they can let their imagination flow more freely when they give themselves permission to write all over the page and in no particular order. If this appeals to you, you might want to consider using several different colors of ink or even crayons. Let yourself draw pictures or insert images if you want—whatever it takes to get your creative juices flowing. The sections below will provide you with guidance as to making your own dream list.

WHEN I WAS A KID ...

It is often easiest to start with a list of the things you thought you wanted to do when you were a child. Did you want to be a musician? Write it down. Did you want to be president? Write it down. Did you want to sail the seven seas? Write it down. Did you want to be many things? Write them all down.

Do not limit yourself to the large dreams you had as a child. If, while watching your mom in the kitchen you thought you would like to own your own bakery or restaurant, write it down. If you loved playing in the dirt or counting stones, write it down.

Let Mildred Council's story inspire you. Known to many as Mama Dip, she is today a successful cookbook author and restaurant owner. But it was not always this way. She is the granddaughter of a slave, and her father was a sharecropper. Her mother died when Mildred was not quite two

> *Don't just let your business or your job make something for you, let it make something of you.*
> —Jim Rohn

years old. As soon as she could, she started helping in the kitchen. She then began doing all the cooking for her father and her six brothers and sisters who all worked in the fields.

Lack of measuring spoons taught her what she calls, "dump cooking." She just poured ingredients into the pot or bowl.

"The only spoon we had in the kitchen was like a teaspoon you use for dessert or drinking coffee," she said. "We didn't have four or five measuring spoons on a little ring hanging up. It wasn't there."

Cooking became her source of employment. She was a cook for three university fraternity houses, two sorority houses, a university dining hall, the Carolina Inn, and in a variety of private homes. Finally she was able to open her own restaurant—dump cooking all the way.

In 1985, *New York Times* food critic Craig Claiborne tried her restaurant and sampled almost every vegetable offered. According to Council, "After about three weeks, he called me and said to me he wanted the recipe for different things, like tomatoes and chicken livers that he was so fond of and black-eyed peas, and I gave it to him. He said, 'Why don't you write these recipes down?'"

Dump cooking doesn't lend itself to written recipes, and it took her another fourteen years to figure out the right way to record her cooking style. Finally, after fits and starts, she began writing down how she cooked, by hand, as she cooked each dish. The University of North Carolina Press published the long-awaited *Mama Dip's Kitchen*.

Although "the book was one of the hardest challenges of my life," according to Council, it has been a huge success leading to her appearance on the Food Network's "Cooking Live" show.

Council has a vision for her restaurant—she wants it to be a place where her children can work to build on the business she started some twenty-five year ago. You can bet she is in touch with and following through on her dreams today.[38]

I'VE THOUGHT ABOUT ...

Write down a list of any business or self-employment opportunity you have ever considered as an adult. Again, do not censor yourself at all. Even if it is something you know you would never seriously consider, it needs to be listed here.

For instance:

- Have you ever thought you could run the place where you work better than the current owners or managers? Write it down.
- Has anyone ever presented you with a multi-level or network marketing opportunity? Write it down.
- Have you ever had a service like carpet cleaning or car washing and thought, "I could do this and do it better"? Write it down.
- Have you ever imagined seeing your name on a tall building, or have you ever seen yourself getting or giving awards? Write it all down.

Let your mind soar. What you are doing is giving yourself permission to let your dreams come forward so you can begin to create a vision of what you really want to do.

Now, next to each business idea write down what attracted you to it. Is it the money? Is it something you always wanted to do? Is it something you are good at? Do you see an opportunity to provide a product or service that had not been created yet? Is it the challenge of doing something that people said was impossible? Do you have a creative idea of how to make something better? Write it all down.

Your list might look something like this:

Business Idea	What I like about it
Multi-level marketing	The money, but …
Owning a horse ranch	Freedom and I love horses
The gadget I invented	I know this would sell
Carpet cleaning	Looks easy and would give lots of freedom

IF I COULD START OVER ...

Another approach is to ask yourself, knowing what you do now, what you would do differently if you were starting your adult life over again. All sorts of things may appear. Some people discover they should have taken up the offer to go into business with a good friend or relative who later went on to be financially successful. Some people wish they had made a different choice when they first were offered a job, and some discover they wish they had taken a different path within their current industry. Some wish they had moved. Others wish they hadn't.

Again, do not limit yourself with practical notions like, "I didn't really have a choice," "My parent's pushed me in this direction," or "If I'd done that, I might be broke today." Just be honest with yourself about the things you might do differently if you were given a chance to start over.

Remember, the whole purpose of all these lists is to put you in touch with your dreams. Your dreams provide valuable clues to the business you want to run. After all, if you are going to start your own business, you want it to be something you truly enjoy doing. It is important that you know this list will be analyzed later, but right now the exercise is merely the making of a list.

CHAPTER 7

CREATE YOUR PERFECT DAY

Immense power is acquired by assuring yourself in your secret reveries that you were born to control affairs.
Andrew Carnegie

Once you have a couple of lists under your belt, it is time to describe to yourself exactly what your perfect working day would be like. You need at least an hour, and you need privacy and quiet to do this exercise well. In fact, it may well be that you need several hours scattered over several days or even a week or two. You want to be totally free to picture exactly how you would like to spend your time if the choice was totally yours.

Answer these questions and add anything else that occurs to you:

- What time would you get up?
- Where would you be when you were working?
- How you would get to work?
- Who would be working with you?
- What resources would you need?
- What kinds of activities do you most enjoy doing while you are working?
- Who would you interact with and how?

- What results would you want from your perfect day?
- What time would you go to bed?
- What would you have liked to accomplish?

Here is how someone who would like to be a freelance writer described their perfect day:

> I'd get up at first light, make coffee for myself, feed my cat, and spend thirty minutes or so doing yoga. Then, walking into my office I'd open the curtains, letting in lots of light and a good view of my garden. I'd turn on my computer, scan my email, check my calendar, and begin to write on the project that took the most creativity.
>
> After a couple of hours, I'd go back to my email, turn on my phone, and spend maybe fifteen minutes dealing with routine stuff. Then back to the computer to spend another hour or two on the project I'd begun in the morning.
>
> I'd break for lunch, which I'd eat in my garden if the weather was good, making sure I took a full hour to relax and refresh myself.
>
> After lunch I'd go back to my computer and work on projects requiring less creativity, including answering emails, a bit of marketing, etc.
>
> I'd end the day knowing I'd put in three or four truly creative hours and an hour or two, or maybe more, depending, on maintaining and building my business. It's during that afternoon time I'd meet with clients over the phone or face-to-face.

> The key to my perfect day is the uninterrupted
> creative time in light-filled surroundings plus
> time to work on the details of my business.[39]

Your perfect day will, of course, be very different from the example above. The first time you do this exercise, it will help you understand yourself a bit better. For example, you will probably get insights into such things as whether or not you really want to work at home, how you feel about commuting, the kinds of people you want to surround yourself with, the pace you like, and what sorts of things bring you the most satisfaction.

Your design of your perfect day will also help you begin to define the kind of business you really want.

MORE LISTS

Now we are going to get a bit more practical with these lists. Don't worry—we will pull all this information together before long.

LIST YOUR HOBBIES

Make a list of your hobbies—those things you like to do in your spare time. List them all, no matter how silly or trivial they may seem.

The reason you should list your hobbies or the way you spend what extra time you have is because those activities contain clues to your dreams and, ultimately, the business you want to start.

> *What would you attempt to do if you could not fail?*
> —Robert Schuller

Sometimes this will be obvious, as in the case of the man who loved to make pottery. When he realized he could start his own pottery studio, he was on his way.

Other examples will not be so clear. For example, if you really like watching football all weekend, you will have to dig a bit deeper. Maybe you will discover you want to open a sports shop of some sort. Sometimes, however, you will find you are actually wasting time with some hobbies because you are unhappy with your work. It could be that when you find and pursue your dream, football watching will become way less important. Be open to whatever you discover.

LIST YOUR SKILLS

This is the place to brag about what you know. Skills fall into multiple categories. For example, a skill may be something physical, like knowing how to build a tree house or how to fix an engine.

Skills also include things like how you deal with people, if you are good with numbers, if you are good at seeing the big picture, or if you are more comfortable with the details.

You may want to ask your spouse, a good friend, or a work colleague for some help with your skills list. Oftentimes other people will recognize skills we do not think of.

For example, while on a flight to Canada I met a fellow who is now a successful seminar leader, and he didn't understand his speaking skills

> *No dream comes true until you wake up and go to work.*
> —Anonymous

were exceptional until someone pointed it out to him. As he tells it, "Speaking to groups has always been pretty easy for me, and I just assumed it was easy for everyone. I truly didn't know I had a special talent."[40]

If you decide to ask someone for help, you do not have to tell them you are thinking of starting your own business. Just ask them what they think you are good at—if they want to know why, tell them you are just curious or are working on a path to self-discovery and just let them talk. You will probably be pleasantly surprised.

LIST YOUR WORK EXPERIENCE

Here you are looking for things you actually have experience with on your job, not your official job title. If, like so many people, you've had several jobs, it may be helpful to put each job title at the top of a single page and then list what you actually did during your time at that job.[41]

For example, a young lady I met while traveling was a technical writer and discovered she did several things that were not in her job description, including:

- Looking at the layout of the manuals to make sure the information flowed visually—what might be called information design. This recognition led to working with the graphic artists and the web designers.
- Technical writing means learning how to talk with software and hardware engineers to get information in a form usable by laypeople. Translating difficult concepts into common language is a skill needed in many occupations.
- Running a focus group to discover what the general public thought about a software product. Again, her ability to interact with the general public opened up all sorts of ideas for starting her own business.

Each of these items involved skills beyond what is usually thought of as technical writing, and each offered clues about proficiencies that might be used in many businesses.

As you list your skills and talents, you will likely delightfully surprise yourself and discover you know how to do well many more things than you ever suspected.

LOOK FOR COMMONALITIES

First of all, take a moment to congratulate yourself for doing such a great job making lists. Now take your lists and read through them looking for commonalities.

You may be surprised to discover, for example, that your childhood dream of being a restaurant owner shows up on several of your lists as something like being good at cooking or being able to wow your friends with good recipes. Perhaps your love for your woodworking hobby points you in a direction of starting a woodworking business offering custom-made doors and windows

Think too about the sorts of advice people are apt to ask you for. Most of us find we have an area or two of expertise we had not suspected. Maybe you are the one in the office people turn to when they have computer problems even though your official job title is something entirely different. There may well be clues to your future business hidden there.

> *Cherish your visions and you dreams, as they are the children of your soul; the blueprints of your ultimate achievements.*
> —Napoleon Hill

Look over your lists again and make note of those things that you really, truly enjoy—for within those things we take pleasure in is often information pointing us toward the business we ultimately want to start.

LISTEN TO THAT LITTLE VOICE INSIDE OF YOU

As you are working with your lists, pay particular attention to that still, small, positive voice inside you. Each of us has within us a part that knows when we are on the right track or not. Some call it intuition, others call it a gut feeling, and still others may recognize it as a hunch. Some experience a physical sensation, maybe in the stomach, the chest, or even the forehead. Others experience it as a knowing or certainty.

However it works for you, when you are working with your lists pay particular attention to that sense or voice. It will guide you as you begin your search.

INFORM YOUR DREAMING

Of course, finding the right business to start is usually more than a matter of making lists, although your lists can reveal the perfect business for you. You also need information, so after you have worked with your lists for awhile, it is time to begin informing yourself about what kinds of businesses there are that might suit you.

There are all sorts of business opportunities out there—everything from the obvious franchises in fast foods, crafts, or carpet cleaning to things like horse ranching, coffee shops or carts, and stage set design. Your next task is to begin to get a feel for the kind of business you would like to start. You are not making a decision at this point, just exploring and learning.

TOOLS TO FIND YOUR DREAM BUSINESS

Below are listed the four best ways to begin informing yourself about the kind of businesses that are out there:

1. Look in the classified section of your favorite big newspaper under *Businesses for Sale* or *Business Opportunities*. You will get the biggest selection on Sunday, and you can do this research with the physical paper and a cup of coffee or over the internet at the newspaper's Web site. Just look at what is available.

   If there is something listed that you find really interesting, ask for more information but be careful. Some of these ads are actually placed by business brokers and are designed to generate leads. That's okay, except at this point you really only want information, not a sales pitch. Write down any ads that seem interesting.

2. Google, "business for sale." Don't get overwhelmed—there are millions of pages. Just read down the first few pages. Mostly you will find brokers of one sort or another offering businesses for sale. Notice that some are companies that seem to work across the whole world, others specialize in a particular area or country, and still others focus on a particular kind of business.

   Go ahead and explore some of the brokers' sites. Notice first just how many different types of businesses there are out there! Try some advanced searches in categories you think you might be interested in. Write down those that intrigue you.

   If you have spotted a couple of types of businesses that you are interested in, try another Google search like this: *<name of business> business for sale*. In many cases, you will find actual businesses in that category for sale.

3. Another place to look for ideas for a business is the yellow pages—just flipping through the pages may trigger an idea you have never thought of. Write down those that interest you.

4. Look through magazines like *Entrepreneur, Inc., Fortune Small Business*, etc. You will find both businesses for sale plus all sorts of information about starting and running your own shop.

THE REAL ROLE OF A BUSINESS BROKER

Be aware that a business broker is much like a real estate broker. They get paid a commission, usually 15 percent, by the seller of a business when the sale is complete. Their job is to sell the businesses they have listed.

If you talk with them directly, they will ask all sorts of questions designed to figure out if you are a hot prospect or not. These qualifying questions include trying to find out if you have enough money to buy a business and how quickly you want to make such a purchase.

If they think you have enough money to buy a business, they will next ask you to sign a confidentiality form and that is okay—they use this form to protect the seller against you sharing with others the financial information they are going to send you.

When you are investigating, feel free to tell the broker you have enough money to invest and go ahead and sign the confidentiality agreement. Your goal is to get as much information as you can, and the confidentiality agreement does not commit you to anything except not sharing the financial information.

Always keep in mind that business brokers get paid a commission only when the sale of a business is completed. This means you are not their number-one priority, and nor do you have their loyalty. You may want to deal with a broker, but just be aware of all the facts.

It is important to note that most of the resources listed in the points above are about businesses you can buy. Although buying an existing business is certainly one option, it is not the only option you have. There are many good reasons to become an entrepreneur by starting your own business from scratch. The purpose of exploring these resources is to give yourself a real taste of the huge variety of businesses out there and to begin to zero in on the type of business you would like to start and own.

GETTING SERIOUS

After you have made your lists, looked for trends and traits in those lists, and explored the amazing variety of businesses out there, it is time to start getting serious about exactly the kind of business you want for yourself.

Obviously, this is a highly personal decision and not one to be taken lightly or made quickly. But it is time to commit, at least to yourself, that you will become an entrepreneur.

When searching for a business, cast your net as wide as you can—you never know what type of opportunity you may come across. Your initial goal is to come up with a list of twenty to twenty-five businesses you think you might like to buy or start.

Begin a more thorough but brief investigation of each business on your list. Talk to people who own a business like the one you are interested in. Look up the business on the internet. Talk to a business broker or two. Ask the broker if the business has certified financials available for review, why the business is for sale, how long the seller would be willing to stay on for training, and if owner financing is an option.

Usually you will discover you want to eliminate most of them for one reason or another. Do not hesitate to throw some options out. Ultimately you want to narrow your search to five.

These businesses are the ones you want to investigate thoroughly. This is a more lengthy process. You want to get a sense of how they work, what it takes to be a success, and your own gut response.

By the time you begin investigating your five possible businesses, you will probably have a pretty good idea of what sort of business you really want. Start focusing there.

If, after completing these exercises, the kind of business has not become clear to you, don't worry. Take a week off and then again go through your lists and all the notes you kept. Add to your lists as things occur to you. It may take several passes before you begin to understand exactly the kind of business you want to start. Once you do understand, go for it.

CHAPTER 8

FORTUNE FAVORS THE BOLD

We have forty million reasons for failure, but not a single excuse.
Rudyard Kipling

Fortune truly favors the bold. You have only to look at a story like Ted Turner's to see how his willingness to take risks resulted in a massive fortune.

Turner's empire building started when he was only twenty-four and he took over his father's billboard business. The business was generating a decent living, but Turner wanted more. Seven years later, he purchased an Atlanta TV station, which became the beginning of the Turner Broadcasting System. Folks thought he was crazy and was taking a huge risk when he launched CNN (Cable News Network), but his vision revolutionized the news industry. Today it is hard to believe, but twenty-four-hour news and our ability to see news almost as it happens is a relatively new phenomenon.[42]

Turner could have stayed with the billboard business—that would have entailed no risk and would have been the safe thing for him to do. Instead, he took risks and has reaped huge rewards as well as changing our understanding of broadcast news.

IT'S EASY TO PLAY IT SAFE

What first appears on the surface as a bold move may not be so bold in hindsight. We tend to see some people as bold or risk takers, yet those people may just have a clearer understanding of the consequences of not taking that leap of faith.

One reason it is so easy to not take risks is that it seems safe. Maybe you have a job, and even if you do not like it much, it is predictable. You know how much you will make each month, and

> *To be a great champion you must believe you are the best. If you're not, pretend you are.*
> —Muhammad Ali

even if you are barely getting by, at least you have some sort of security ... or do you?

Downsizing, rightsizing, outsourcing, and merger mania make every job today inherently insecure. Where once many American employees had something close to job security; that is simply no longer true—nor does it appear it ever will be true again.

What is strange is even those who lose their jobs often go right back into the job market looking for something similar. Why do so many people do this? Because it is human nature to seek out things we are comfortable with even if the results are negative.

Yet how easy is it, really, to do something day after day you truly do not like and that does not support your future? Henry David Thoreau said it best:

Most men lead lives of quiet desperation and go to the grave with the song still in them.

Are you truly singing your song, or are you a bit stuck?

Is Life Passing You By?

If you are still working a job and do not have specific plans toward moving into owning your own business or at least actively exploring how you can start your own business, you are stuck. There are many symptoms of being stuck. Ask yourself if you are guilty of any of the following:

- Wishing your job and life were different but not doing anything about it.
- Dreaming about owning your own business but having a million excuses about why now is not the time.
- Wanting your own business but listening to those who say you should stay where you are.
- Spending months and months exploring having your own business but taking no action beyond that.
- Spending hours and hours planning how you will make your move but not taking any real action or setting firm dates to do so.
- Talking about starting your own business, but only talking.
- Waiting until the time is right without defining exactly how you will know the moment when it arrives.

If you checked off any of the above, be honest with yourself. What are you going to do about it?

Boldness Is Required

There is no doubt about it—starting your own business requires boldness and a willingness to take risks. Consider this example of boldness:

When Jeong Kim sold his telecommunications business to Lucent Technologies for 1.1 billion dollars, he was only thirty-seven years old.

What is not obvious at first are the obstacles he had to overcome. Kim arrived in the U.S. when he was fourteen, barely able to speak English, and lived with his family in subsidized housing in Maryland.

By the time he was sixteen he had moved into the basement of his high school math teacher and was supporting himself with several jobs, including the night shift at a 7-Eleven. He graduated from high school a semester early and began saving for college.

A year later, he applied and was accepted to Johns Hopkins University, and he attended using his savings and some financial aid. There, in addition to his studies, Kim worked at a technology start-up full time.

After graduation he joined the Navy. "In a 2006 interview of Kim by achievements.org, Kim said, "I wanted to pay back society. Maybe that's idealistic, but it felt right."

He served on a nuclear submarine for seven years, and he learned about leadership. "When you're surrounded 24/7 by 120 other people, you learn to appreciate other views," he said.

It was during his duty on submarines that Kim developed his central business strategy. "I tend to say less and do more," he said. "In a nuclear submarine, we call it silent service. A show of force is not our mission. Our job is to be very effective."

In the Navy, Kim came to understand a telecommunications-switching problem that became the basis for his future business. He also completed his master's in Business Administration at Johns Hopkins.

Following his stint in the Navy, Kim joined Allied Signal, and while working there full time completed a doctorate in Engineering at the University of Maryland.

In 1992, Kim struck out on his own as a consultant. It took more than a year for him to land his first contract. That seventy-five thousand-dollar nuclear safety assessment deal gave him enough money to continue working on his switching technology.

It was not until 1997 that he introduced his new switching technology, quickly selling thousands of switches to companies like AT&T and Verizon and landing his company, Yurie Systems, on the cover of *Business Week*.

Jeong Kim did not have as many opportunities as you and I probably have. Yet he acted with boldness, displaying a quality that used to be known as "having grit." He acted boldly and continued to press on.[43]

This is why my own personal motto is:

> ***Small Risk Small Gain,***
> ***Big Risk Big Gain,***
> ***No Risk No Gain.***

Is Boldness Natural?

Some people seem born to take risks, whereas others are not. Can you learn to become comfortable with taking risks? Yes. Although at times learning to take risks may seem like turning an aircraft carrier around, it can be done. Like the carrier, you can create your own boldness with small course corrections, continuing until you have reached your new course heading—boldness.

Those who seem unwilling to take risks have simply lost touch with their own natural boldness. Perhaps their parents overprotected them in the name of keeping them safe and they have unconsciously adopted that same attitude. Maybe people around them are continually urging them to stay safe and not strike out on their own. Whatever the reason, those truly are only excuses.

Many other people are relatively fearless in parts of their lives and timid about other things.

Take, for example, the office worker who bravely participates in rock climbing or hang gliding and yet cringes at the thought of starting her own business out of fear of failing. Or take the mechanic who, while demonstrating over and over again he knows more than his boss and urging the shop to use the newest technology, stays as an employee because it feels safe. All these people need to do is transfer their willingness to risk something in one area of their lives into the willingness to risk starting their own business.

Everyone can learn to access their own natural boldness so they can take the necessary risks to becoming a successful entrepreneur.

Are You a Risk Taker?

Deep down, the answer is yes, but sometimes that is hard to see. There are all sorts of quizzes to help you determine if you have what it takes to be an entrepreneur. The problem with most of them is that if you score low, you are left with the feeling that you should not start your own business. However, those tests only reveal areas you will have to work on a bit harder—they are actually guides to discovering what you need to know in order to start your own business.

Below is a similar quiz but with a major difference. The goal here is to figure out what changes you may need to make in your own attitude to increase your risk tolerance so you can confidently become an entrepreneur. Rate yourself on each question from zero to five, with five being the highest:

___ Are you a self-starter? Would you say you are highly motivated?

If you score less than three, pay particular attention to the section on finding dreams. Are you disciplined?

If you decide you are not very disciplined, pay particular attention to the list of reasons why you want to start your own business.

__ Do you mostly complete the important tasks you set for yourself?

Double check yourself on this one—the key is to recognize the difference between important tasks and tasks that are urgent but not important.

__ Are you capable of hard work?

Be careful not to rate yourself too low here—all of us are capable of hard work if we see the point in it.

__ Are you reasonably well-organized?

Before you score yourself on this one, know that the key here is not neat files or a tidy desk—the real point is to understand if you can keep track of lots of things and find what you need to find when you need to find it—most of the time.

__ Can you keep trying even when there is no guarantee of success?

Again, the chances are you are willing to try when you know what you are working toward is worth the effort. Review your dreams and reasons for starting your own business before answering this one.

__ Do you have a good support network—spouse, relatives, friends, etc.—or are you willing to get one?

No one succeeds in their own business totally on their own. You either need to start with a good support network or be willing to acquire one.

__ Are you a problem solver?

Before you are tempted to rate yourself lower than four or five, make a list of the problems, big and little, you solve during a typical day. Chances are you are a problem solver. We all are, but often we do not recognize it.

__ Are you willing to make decisions?

Before you answer this one, read the next section.

Take the First Step

The simple truth is starting your own business begins with taking action and deciding you will change your life. That is the beginning. No one ever took a risk without first deciding to take that risk.

Get off the fence and make your decision with conviction. It cannot be wishy-washy or couched in terms like, "Some day I'll start my own business." Your decision must be accompanied by determination and willingness. In fact, it can be said:

**Decision +
Determination =
Boldness**

Look at the risks you have already taken

One way to develop comfort with risk is to list the risks you have already taken in your life. Such a list might begin like this:

1. I learned to play _____ ____(a sport, an instrument, etc.).
2. I bought my first home.
3. I learned to drive a car.
4. I got married.
5. I got divorced.
6. I had a child.
7. I moved to a new city.
8. I changed careers.

9. I asked my boss for a raise.
10. I gave my first company presentation.
11. I headed up a committee.

We all take risks, big ones and small ones, every day. Once you have made your list, look over it and pick out one or two items. Remember how you felt before you started a risky activity? Do you remember, for example, how scary it was the first time you rode your bike without training wheels? Do you remember how scary it was the first time you drove without the driving instructor? How about the first time you applied for a job?

Each is an example of your willingness to take risks. You see? You do have the ability to risk starting your own business! You just need to access that skill again.

PRACTICE TAKING RISKS

You can actually begin to train yourself to be a risk taker. It starts with taking small risks or baby steps toward the bigger goal of starting your own business. Exactly how to practice risk taking varies from person to person, but the following suggestions should fuel your imagination.

- Drive to work a different way at least once a week. The risk here might be arriving late or getting lost, but do it anyway for practice.
- Talk with three people who are in business for themselves. The risk here might be feeling foolish or having the sense that there is no point in it. Do it anyway and see what you discover.
- Call three business brokers. Tell them about your dream business and see what they have to say. Remember, business brokers are salespeople, so do not let yourself get sold at this point. The risk is feeling foolish or like you should know more

than you do. Do it anyway and listen carefully to what they have to say.

- Try a new restaurant that serves a kind of food you have never tried before. The risk is you won't like what you order. If you have been bold enough to go to a restaurant where they speak a different language, you also risk not even understanding what you are ordering. That is okay because you may discover something you really like.
- If you always pack your lunch, one day a week eat out. If you always eat out for lunch, one day a week pack your own lunch.
- Sleep on the other side of the bed and see how it feels.
- Buy a piece of clothing that is unlike what you normally wear and wear it in public.
- Alter your morning routine—if you normally drink coffee, try tea or switch from bacon and Eggo waffles to oatmeal.
- Take a day off for no reason at all.

You get the idea. Make a practice of doing something different from your normal routine. Make at least mental notes of what you are doing, what you are risking, and what it feels like. Notice how often you feel good about the risk you just took. Congratulate yourself on becoming a risk taker.

CHALLENGE YOUR FEARS

Another way to practice risk taking is to challenge yourself about any fears you know you have. For instance:

- Are you afraid of heights? Go bungee jumping— if that is too much to start with, find baby steps in between until you can bungee jump.

- Do you avoid public speaking because of fear? Join Toastmasters and stick with it until you can face an audience with confidence.
- Are you single but hesitant to ask someone out? Do it anyway.
- Are you afraid to dance in public? Sign up for a dance class.
- Does flying make you quake? Make arrangements to take a trip in a small plane and talk with the pilot about your fears.
- Have you always wanted to paint, draw, take photographs, or work with pottery but think you do not have any talent? Take a class, a workshop, or both!

Every single time you challenge one of your fears, you are getting back in touch with your natural risk-taking ability. Not only will this help you assume the risk of starting your own business, but you will also find you are living your life in a larger, more exciting way.

A WORD ABOUT COMFORT ZONES

You are probably familiar with the idea of your comfort zone. It is often presented as a circle, and inside the circle are all of the things you are familiar with and comfortable doing.

Outside the circle is usually considered outside your comfort zone.[44] Those things outside your comfort zone are areas that feel risky. But that is not the whole truth. We actually operate out of at least two nested circles. The center circle is all that is familiar and comfortable—our Comfort Zone.

The outer circle is our Learning and Excitement Zone—it is just outside our Comfort Zone and in fact overlaps it. It also overlaps the area outside our Comfort Zone.

This outside area could also be called our Risk Zone, for it is here, in the Learning and Excitement Zone, that we find the energy to break out of our rut and start our own business. It is overlapping with our Comfort Zone because we constantly draw on what we know to inform the new actions we take. Every time you challenge yourself, you have moved into the Learning and Excitement Zone.

The most exciting part of all this is that after a time we become comfortable with the Learning and Excitement Zone and it fades into and enlarges our Comfort Zone, giving us ever more opportunity to expand and live life in large and expansive ways. In effect, we keep expanding our Learning and Excitement Zone as we more fully embrace life.

As you probably guessed, starting your own business is done mostly in the Learning and Excitement Zone. That is where you want to be.

Take a moment to read and reflect on this poem on following your dream.

To laugh is to risk appearing a fool.
To weep is to risk appearing sentimental.
To reach out for another is to risk involvement.
To expose feelings is to risk exposing your true self.

To place your ideas, your dreams, before the crowd is to risk their loss.
To love is to risk not being loved in return.
To live is to risk dying.
To hope is to risk despair.
To try is to risk failure.

But risks must be taken because the greatest hazard in life is to risk nothing.
The person who risks nothing … does nothing … has nothing … is nothing.
You may avoid suffering and sorrow, but you simply cannot learn, feel, change, grow, love … live.
Chained by your certitudes, you are a slave—you have forfeited freedom.

Only a person who risks is free.
(Author unknown)

CHAPTER 9

TRY, TRY AGAIN

Our greatest glory is not in never failing, but in rising up every time we fail.
Ralph Waldo Emerson

There is a single attribute that guarantees success, and it may surprise you. It is not intelligence, education, being born to wealth, genetics, or where you were born. No, it is none of these. And it isn't luck either.

Simply put, the single characteristic that will make you a success in your own business is persistence.

The American Heritage Dictionary defines being persistent as: *refusing to give up.*

Yep, it is just that simple. If you want to succeed as an entrepreneur, you must be willing to try, try, and try again. History is full of examples of how persistence and tenacity pays off.

EDISON KEEPS TRYING

Consider Thomas Edison, who contributed so much to our modern way of life. Known as the Wizard of Menlo Park, he developed what can be considered the first industrial research laboratory and brought the principles of mass production to the invention process. As a result, he created:

- The first incandescent light bulb
- The first telephone
- The first electronic broadcast system with the stock ticker
- The first phonograph
- The first motion picture camera
- The first two-way telegraph

Also, he contributed to the creation of many other inventions that have moved humanity from the industrial age into the age of information.

But Edison was not an instant success—far from it. His development of a practical light bulb, one that would not burn out almost instantly, took him a full eighteen months. Although most histories focus on the carbon filament he created, he also had to create a whole system which would allow for electric lights to replace gas lamps. That system included:

- The parallel circuit
- A durable light bulb
- An improved dynamo
- The underground conductor network
- The devices for maintaining constant voltage
- Safety fuses and insulating materials
- Light sockets with on-off switches

It is unknown exactly how many different methods Edison actually tried before he struck on the ultimately successful idea for the filament. It was at least hundreds and perhaps more. It is worth noting that other scientists had been trying to create a working light bulb for seventy years prior to Edison's success. Each one of them gave up, and Edison persisted until he succeeded.[45]

Passion + *Self-Belief* = *Persistence*

Real tenacity and persistence come from two sources:

- Passion for what you are doing
- Belief in yourself.

It is hard to say which comes first because both are critical. Both are also what might be termed "internal states." That is, neither belief in yourself nor passion for what you do can come from the outside. While it is true that others can support you in your efforts and that sort of support certainly helps, it is ultimately up to you.

One of my favorite stories is about my friend Josiah. Born in London, England, he came to America in 1997. He began investing in real estate when he was twenty-seven years old. Today, he is a multi-millionaire.

When I asked him about his beginnings in real estate, he told me it all started when he began working and fixing things around his mother's house. "I didn't trust the contractors," he said. While he was fixing things, he realized that he was not only repairing but also adding value to the home, so he asked himself, "What if I could do this with other homes?" Without any mentors and no real estate experience, he began to look for fixer-uppers to buy, repair, and rent out.

After successfully investing in England's real estate market, he decided to move to America and apply his investing experience in the U.S. He now lives on a 1.3 million-dollar estate in addition to managing his real estate business.

This would be an amazing story in itself, but what you do not know is that Josiah does all of this from a wheelchair. You see, the day he arrived in Orlando, Florida, he was in an automobile accident which left him paralyzed—he barely has the use of his arms, much less his legs. Still, he continues to build his wealth through investing in real estate.

Josiah has overcome at least three major obstacles:

- He is an African American.
- He is confined to a wheelchair.
- He is from another country.

It is safe to say that Josiah not only found his dream, but he has succeeded at it.

That is why we have spent so much time talking about finding your real dreams. Dreams are the doorway to the kind of passion that will, when coupled with a belief in yourself, fuel the persistence you need. The exercises in chapter 6, *Dream Like A Child—Finding Your Passion*, and chapter 7, *Create Your Perfect Day*, are so important because they put you in touch with your dreams and true passions.

Use these exercises and any others you find in this book to help you get in touch with what you really want.   Chapter 7 also contains some exercises that will help you with your belief in yourself. So does chapter 8, *Fortune Favors the Bold*. As you review what you have done in the past, you will begin to see you are truly a good person with a great deal to give, you have many skills, and you are more than capable of acquiring additional skills and learning new things.

A WORD ABOUT FOLLOW-THROUGH

Implicit in persistence and energy is follow-through. Follow-through can be defined simply as: *doing what you promise.*

Promises tend to fall into two categories:

1. Promises you make to others.
2. Promises you make to yourself.

Promises you make to others is the most obvious area of follow-through for the successful entrepreneur. Anything you promise you must deliver. It is far better not to promise than to break a promise.

Less obvious, but perhaps even more important, are the promises we make to ourselves. A wise and a successful business person will think carefully before promising themselves anything.

Think about it. How often have you said, "I'll lose weight," "I'll save more," or "I'll spend more time with my family" and then failed to take action on that self-promise?

When you fail to follow through with yourself, you are building a pattern of failure. It is far better not to make those promises so easily. Instead, consider carefully what you are saying. Ask yourself such questions as:

- Is this something I really want?
- Or is it simply something I think I should want?
- Assuming I really want it, what will I actually have to do to follow through?
- Is there something I need to do first so I'll be able to follow through?
- How will I feel about it and myself if I *don't* follow through?
- How will I feel about it and myself if I *do* follow through?

Answering these questions puts you in a position to only make promises to yourself that you are likely to keep. Keeping promises to yourself builds self-esteem and success, and after a while it becomes a positive habit that will serve you well as you start and develop your own business.

The truth is you do have what it takes to be a successful entrepreneur, including the ability to try, try, and try again. It simply takes some effort.

So What If I Fail?

First of all, what, exactly, do you mean by failure? It is important to distinguish between setbacks and failure. Anyone in business for themselves will experience setbacks as well as successes. A setback is not failure.

But supposing you fail completely and have to shut your business down? What does that actually mean to you? Your attitude here is critical.

Each setback and failure brings you closer and closer to success if you choose to frame it that way.

The one certainty that will keep you from achieving your goal of success is to quit trying. Do not be a quitter.

Nina Vaca was brought to Los Angeles when she was two years old. Her parents came to the U.S. so they could build a family business.

"My father believed that the key to the American dream was through entrepreneurship," Vaca said.

Hernan Vaca began by opening a travel business, which he later expanded to three offices. His goal was to eventually have five offices—one for each of his children. When they were young, Nina and her siblings would take the bus after school to work in the agency.

Nina had just graduated from high school when her father was killed during a robbery at his travel agency. Almost overwhelmed, Nina and her older sister, Jessica, ran the business and got it ready for sale.

Once the travel agency had sold, Nina headed for Texas State University, where she majored in business and graduated in three and a half years. Her first job was in a technology company in New York City. Before long, the company returned her to Texas to head up its Dallas office.

It was during this period that Nina realized she was good at attracting clients. So, at the age of twenty-five she left the security of a

> *It is on our failures that we base a new and different and better success.*
> —Havelock Ellis

regular job and started her own business with a partner. Together they created Pinnacle, a recruiting company designed to recruit high-tech candidates for businesses that needed IT people to administer their computer systems.

"Because of my upbringing, I always took matters into my own hands," Vaca said. "In my gut, I knew I could do this."

In 2001, along with the dot com bust, the whole tech industry took a nosedive. Pinnacle was no exception and, according to Vaca, "was almost down to a liquidation plan."

Her partner wanted out. Vaca said, "I scratched up as much money as I could to buy the business, paying him a little more than the book value of his share."

Accepting the way the market had changed, she changed her company's focus to providing consultants to businesses that were laying off their tech staffs. Rather than charge the standard hourly rate, she charged a fixed fee, which gave companies the ability to predict their expenses.

She was successful with this approach, landing accounts with Verizon, PepsiCo, and other large companies. It is unlikely that her father, Hernan Alfredo Vaca, would have dreamed that by the time she was thirty-four his daughter would be the sole owner of Pinnacle Technical Resources, a tech business expected in 2006 to generate sixty million dollars or more.

Today, Vaca reinvests most of her money in her business with an eye toward making it the family legacy her father dreamed of.

The trick is to use any failure or setback as a learning experience. That is what Nina Vaca did when the dot com boom went bust, and that is what is meant when successful people talk about going to the school of "hard knocks." They did not learn by reading a book or sitting in a classroom! They lived it. They learned through experience. Experience is the greatest teacher.

When you start your own business, you are going to get knocked down. Those failures prepare you for the next experience in your life.

Remember the old adage, "When you get knocked off your horse you need to get right back on and keep riding." If you don't, you will always be afraid.

Persistence and a refusal to accept setbacks and failures as the final word are what will guarantee your success as an entrepreneur.

Now, go do it!

RESOURCES

Web sites

There is an amazing amount of information available for entrepreneurs on the Internet. Not all of it is trustworthy, but here is a list of sites I know and respect.

- **My Wealth Puzzle**—the companion Web site for this and subsequent books.
  http://www.mywealthpuzzle.com, and if you want to order any of the resources online or see what else we recommend, go to our resources page: http://www.mywealthpuzzle.com/resources-movies-books.php
- *Entrepreneur*—the companion Web site for *Entrepreneur Magazine*. http://www.entrepreneur.com
- *Inc.* —the companion Web site for *Inc. Magazine*. http://www.inc.com
- NASE (National Association for the Self Employed)—a self-help organization for entrepreneurs. http://nase.org
- Small Business Administration—government help for small businesses. http://www.sba.gov/
- SCORE—free help for small business through volunteers.

http://www.score.org
- Social Security Administration
  http://www.ssa.gov/
- Entrepreneurs at About.com—a comprehensive site for small business.
  http://entrepreneurs.about.com/

To order additional copies of *Solving the Wealth Puzzle*, please go to www.mywealthpuzzle.com.

(ENDNOTES)

Notes

1 Social Security Administration, www.ssa.gov/history/breifhistory3.html.

2 Employee Benefit Research Institute, www.ebri.org/publication/facts.

3 "The Status of the Medicare HI and SMI Trust Funds: The Trustee's 2006 Annual Report," www.aarp.org/research/medicare.

4 Social Security Administration, www.ssa.gov/history/lifeexpect.

5 Associated Press, news release, February 1, 2007.

6 Money, *USA Today*, "Ford will cut 25,000 to 30,000 jobs," January 23, 2006.

7 Paul Lutus, www.arachnoid.com/stocks/, 2002.

8 Investment Company Institute, news release, Washington, DC, October 18, 2007.

9 Colleen Taylor, "Stock Options gaga claims another NASDAQ veteran," www.edn.com, January 31, 2007.

10 *Wall Street Journal* study done by Thornburg Investment Management, February 2006.

11 Laura Bruce, "Savings rate in America," www.bankrate.com. 03-08-2006

12 Jeanne Sahadi, "Millionaires in America," www.CNNMoney.com, April 17, 2007,

13 Edward Wolff, "Top Heavy: The increasing inequality of wealth in America and what can be done about it," *Multinational Monitor* 24, no. 5 (May 2003).

14 Small Business Administration, Office of Advocacy, "Frequently asked questions," 2007, www.sba.gov.

15 David Futrelle, "Getting Rich in America," CNNMoney. com,

16 The US Bureau of Labor Statistics. www.bls.gov/nls/nlsy 79r19.pdf.

17 http://www.laborradio.org/node/3556

18 Kate Lorenz, "Job Burnout: Symptoms and Remedies," September 24, 2007, www.careerbuilder.com.

19 www.entrepreneurialconnection.com, June 2006

20 Gregory P. Smith, "Top-Ten Reasons Why People Quit Their Jobs," www.businessknowhow.com,

21 Sir Richard Branson, www.wikipedia.org.

22 US Small Business Administration, Office of Advocacy, news release, June 22, 2006, sba.gov.

23 Holly Hendrick Tredway, "17 Easy Steps for Setting Up a Home Based Business," www.articlebase.com, October 30, 2007.

24 Anthony Deemer

25 U.S. Census Bureau, Housing And Household Economics Statistics Division, www.census.gov/hhes/www/poverty, March 10, 2009   National Law Center on Homelessness And Poverty study done 2007, www.nationalhomeless.org , March 10, 2009

26 Center for Women's Business Research, www.cfwbr.org.

27 American Payroll Association, "Getting Paid in America Survey," www.ketknbc.com, October 17, 2007.

28 Katharine Diaz, article on Belinda Guadarrama, www. hispanictrends.com, Spring 2003,

29 Jennifer Errick, "Debt, Security and the American Dream," www.newdream.org,

30 Bill & Melinda Gates Foundation, "Annual Report 2006," www.gatesfoundation.org.

31 Anthony Deemer

32 Scott Allen, "Entrepreneurs Success Story: Brian Scudamore," www.about.com,

33 Bill Gates, www.wikipedia.org.

34 Davide Dukcevich, "College vs No College," www.Forbes.com, July 20, 2003, LINK NEEDED.

35 Colonel Sanders, www.wikipedia.org.

36 Matthew Miller, "America's 400 Richest," www.Forbes.com, September 21, 2006, LINK NEEDED.

37 *Forbes Magazine*, "The Richest 400," 2006.

38 *Small Business Week*, "2002 Winners," http://app.sba.gov/sbsuccess/2002/dsp_winner_info.cfm.

39 Anthony Deemer

40 Anthony Deemer

41 Anthony Deemer

42 Ted Turner, www.wikipedia.org.

43 Jeong Kim, www.achievement.org

44 Anthony Deemer

45 Thomas Edison, www.wikipedia.org.

www.ingramcontent.com/pod-product-compliance
Lightning Source LLC
Chambersburg PA
CBHW030815180526
45163CB00003B/1291